To my beloved Joyce —
— glad we've both
been found!

Eugenia Price
Genie

Love, love, love!

Psalm 63:1

Early Will I
Seek Thee

Early Will I

Seek Thee

Journal of a Heart that

Longed and Found

EUGENIA PRICE

FLEMING H. REVELL COMPANY

To My Mother

PREFACE

Longing, natural to us all, leads to—*seeking*. God did not create us as a Divine pastime. He created us to *find* that for which we seek. Jesus said: "Seek and ye shall find."

It is my belief that every man or woman or young person in the world is longing for something more of life. Some do not realize this, but I believe it is true, just the same.

And longing leads naturally to seeking.

Jesus could say, "Seek and ye shall find," because He knew we were being *sought*! He, Himself, was seeking us for Himself. He, Himself, is still seeking us for Himself.

When we receive Him, we find.

We find because we are *found*.

And once we have been found by the One who Himself is our destiny, a new and deeper kind of longing is set up which does not leave us dis-satisfied, but which leaves us forever *unsatisfied*.

The more we see of His Face, the more we want of Him.

The more we know Him, the more we long to know Him.

I believe the longing heart is shared by those who are and those who are not followers of Jesus Christ. This book is a journal of sharing my own longing and finding. And of being

7

found. It is written because I believe He Himself is the end of *everyman's* search.

For the time required to read *Early Will I Seek Thee,* will you lay aside whatever might throw a shadow between you as you are and Jesus Christ as He is?

Even if you have tried "religion" and feel a failure . . . even if you are "sure of your doctrine" and are dry in that certainty . . . even if you still do not believe God revealed Himself *only* in the Lord Jesus Christ, expose yourself as you *are* to Him as He *is,* for these few pages and leave the results with Him.

Even if you are already *one* with Him, there is more for you. There is more for me.

This is a book for all longing hearts everywhere.

Eugenia Price

Chicago, Illinois
January, 1956

CONTENTS

9

INTRODUCTION

If you are self-satisfied, you will not be interested in this book. But read it anyway, and you will see what you are missing.

If we are self-satisfied, we can never know the supreme joy of being Christ-satisfied, of having our every need and desire fulfilled in Him. We read in the Scriptures, "Our sufficiency is of God," not realizing what immensely practical results it could and should have in our everyday lives.

This book is primarily for the wistful, eager heart—weary, as it were, of the copies, longing for the Original.

Once more Genie Price brings us to our Saviour, removing the confusion of thought that so often enshrouds Him, so that we see Him as He is—right beside us, invisible to our mortal eyes but infinitely more real than we are, the source of our longing and its satisfaction.

I consider it a privilege to recommend to your thoughtful and prayerful reading a book which has already meant so much to me.

Ruth Bell Graham

Early Will I
Seek Thee

1. GOD CREATED LONGING!

If you long for nothing as you begin this book, you are either dead or deceived!

This is not an attack on your ability to have built a successful and satisfactory life for yourself. It is no attack on the merits of your family, or your state of mind. If you are a believer in Jesus Christ, neither is this an attack on your spiritual status.

I merely believe longing is natural with us all.

I believe our longing is simply the *result* of God's original intention toward us. He made us in His Own image. He made us with a capacity for the highest enjoyment. He made us with a capacity to enjoy Himself! There can be no joy higher. Because there is no one higher than God.

". . . for I am God, and there is none else."

God's original intention toward us has not changed at all. He still wants the *very best* for each one of us. If your heart longs for higher ground in any area of your

15

life, from your work to your personal relationships with your family and those you love, this is all God's idea!

He planted longing in us when He created us.

Our capacity to desire comes from the very *desire* in God's Own heart.

Then what went wrong?

Why has the word *longing* come to mean misery?

Why has the word *longing* come to mean frustration and loneliness?

Why, instead of associating a longing heart with the potential of the promised joy up ahead, do we invariably *sigh* when we remember our longing heart?

Is God's original intention really still the same?

Does He still want to fulfill us?

Yes, He does.

". . . I am come that they might have life, and that they might have it more abundantly."

"These things have I spoken unto you, that my joy might remain in you, and that your joy might be full."

". . . seek and ye shall find. . . ."

Then what happened?

Why do we seem to search and still not find?

Do we long for too much?

Should we be satisfied with less?

No.

We belittle God when we beg for crumbs, while He stands before us in the Person of Jesus Christ and declares Himself to be the entire bread of life!

Far from expecting too much, we expect too little.

". . . I am the first, I also am the last."

". . . by him all things consist."

"For it pleased the Father that in him (Jesus) should all fulness dwell."

~~By Him all things consist!~~

~~In Him all fullness dwells!~~

But what does this have to do with our longing?

~~The answer to that question is the theme of this book.~~

It cannot be answered in mere words and yet it is all contained in the startling words of Jesus Christ Himself as He confronts us at this moment, still declaring: ". . . *I* am the way, the truth, and the life. . . ."

In Him is everything.

In Him is everything for which I long.

I may not know it, but it is there.

This is true for Christian and non-Christian alike. We were all made in His image and His highest will for every human being alive today is that He be allowed to fill every longing in every life!

"Behold, I stand at the door, and knock: if any man . . . open the door, I will come in. . . ."

"For it pleased the Father that in him should all fulness dwell."

Therefore, when He comes in, *everything* for which I long is there for me to enjoy!

~~Is this true?~~

~~The Bible says it is.~~

17

Then why are we restless and worried and anxious and filled with longings that are *not* fulfilled?

~~Does God taunt us because we are mere humans?~~

Has He somehow lost His power to keep His promises?

Why is the world filled with people whose lives are empty except for the eternal desire and longing for what they never hope to get?

Are we always to be hungry for our soul's sincere desire?

The Bible says God will fill the hungry with good things.

Is this true?

Yes. God wants to fill us. Jesus Christ still stands declaring: ". . . I am the way, the truth, and the life. . . ." *But* He also still adds that ". . . no man cometh unto the Father, but by *me*."

In *Him* . . . in Jesus Christ Himself do all things consist.

It pleased the Father that in *Him* should all fullness dwell. And that "fullness" *includes* the fulfillment of your own truest longing as you ~~read these lines right~~ now!

"Then," you say, "if I am *not* a Christian I cannot possibly hope to have my longings fulfilled. But if I receive Jesus Christ into my life, then automatically all of my desires are met."

I would have to answer, "No."

18

Because most of our particular desires and longings have become twisted by the sin that entered man *after* God had made man in His Own image. Your desires may be out of God's will for your life. We were made in God's image when He created us, but the selfishness in our own natures twisted our God-given longings into desires He could never grant. And so I could never tell you that you will have everything you *now think* you want if you will become a follower of Jesus Christ.

Sin has so twisted you, if you have never asked Christ to blot out that sin, that the self *you* know you to be has become in one sense a *false* self. Not the one God intended at all. God made us in His image, but we can become so hemmed in by our selfish selves and peer for so many years from our own viewpoint, that we create an altogether different "image" of our selves and begin to live from that false position, thus living against the grain of the universe and against the God who created it!

In other words, we play God.

Re-creating, as it were, an opinionated, pampered, narrow, self-concerned image of ourselves and psychology calls us neurotic.

God will not satisfy your neurotic longings.

He would be a fiend if He did.

But, He did create your *capacity* to long, and I know from my own experience that before I became a Christian I absolutely did not know what my real self was like! So, of course, I didn't know what I really wanted. As a result, eighteen years of my so-called adult life were spent in trying to satisfy longings which were impossible to fulfill! They were sinful, false, self-deceived longings conjured up from my sinful, false, self-centered viewpoint.

God could not grant them.

Jesus Christ is a Saviour, not a destroyer!

If you are not a Christian, you may not believe this, but on the Cross of Calvary, God, who hung there *in* Christ, made all the necessary arrangements, released all the necessary power to re-create that twisted self of yours *back* into His Own image so that your *real* needs and longings and desires *can* be satisfied by Christ Himself.

I do not force my *opinion* upon you in this matter.

I merely share my *experience*.

In the year 1949, at the age of thirty-three, I "opened the door" when the Holy Spirit of this same Jesus Christ began to move upon and move within my empty, twisted, frustrated life. I did not know it was the Holy Spirit then. I would have laughed at the idea, had anyone suggested it. But He was working, just the same. He not only began to attract my attention, He gave me the power to forsake my old life and dare to step out into one so new that I trembled at the very thought of beginning to live in a world populated by people who went

20

to church and understood the Bible and let God guide their lives!

I had never really believed in God at all.

Of course, I trembled. I was well rutted in my false life.

I was familiar there. But, this same Holy Spirit began to put strange, uneasy feelings of a new kind of "homesickness" in my heart and the name of Jesus Christ made my heart beat until I could hear it in my ears at night.

I didn't belong to Him yet, but I wanted to.

I was afraid to let go at first, but I *longed* for Christ Himself.

The very realization of the longing frightened me, but it was there. And it was about to begin to be fulfilled.

When I opened the door, He came in.

And with Him the *beginning* of my first *real* fulfillment. But with Him also came the beginning of my first *real* longing. Longing that came from the heart of God to my heart.

The kind of longing God *can* answer.

Did all my desires change immediately? No, not all of them, by any means. God not only created my mind, He knew, as no one knew, how twisted it had become through the years. He "understood my thought afar off." His eyes saw "my substance." . . . even the substance of my new intentions, "being yet unperfect." In His Book, all my members and intentions and neuroses

21

and notions and self-deceptions were written . . . He knew me.

He knew the real person I *could* be in Christ Jesus.

He knew the false, sinful self which had strangled His purpose in my life for so many years.

Gradually, my desires began to change. I began to long for different things and to experience those new longings fulfilled almost as quickly as they came. He knows exactly how fast to work in new Christians. He knew exactly how rapidly to work with me. And how slowly.

He knows exactly how rapidly to work in you.

And how slowly.

"Such knowledge is too wonderful for me; it is high, I cannot attain unto it."

He knows.

He knows about you as you read.

"But," *you* say, "I *am* a Christian! I *have* received Jesus Christ as my Saviour. I did this many years ago and, oh, how I strive to be a good Christian and obey God! But, in spite of this I'm not fulfilled! This is wrong and that is wrong and sometimes my defeats come so close together I almost doubt that Christ came in at all! What's wrong with me? Why am I so lonely? Why isn't my longing for a companion satisfied? Why do I long to look young and fear getting old?"

Or perhaps yours is *another* longing. Maybe you've had an alcohol problem. Maybe you've sincerely received Jesus Christ as your Saviour and you still have that problem! Do you feel like beating your head against a wall and shouting "Why?" at God?

Perhaps *you* have been trying for t~~hirty-two~~ years to hold your tongue and in spite of all your sincerity toward God and your work in the church and your correct doctrines, you're still "blowing your top" when a certain type of person crosses your path *and you*!

You received Christ. Isn't He in you?

Yes, He is.

He said He would come in. And He is a God of His Word.

Then, what's wrong?

~~Think.~~

Could it be that you have been living your life in compartments? Trusting Christ for your material supply and not trusting Him for the power to lose your temper forever? Trusting Him with your new job, but not really believing He can take the place of that bottle?

Compartments.

Here.

But not *there*.

Could it be that even though you assent intellectually to the *fact* that He did really come in to live in you when you received Him as your Saviour, you have not begun to *act* on that belief?

Intellectually, I believe in the laws of aviation and in the adaptability of the modern airplane to those laws.

23

But I *prove* that belief when I walk calmly aboard and allow a plane to carry me from coast to coast.

Could it be that in *almost* every area of your life you have begun to act on your belief that Christ did come to live His life in you when you received Him? Could you have begun to do this to such a fine extent that most people consider you a spiritual stalwart? And yet, *you* know and God knows about that one area. That one place where you are still not victorious. //

To long for victory in *all facets* of our lives is from God.

Constantly He is urging us to come up a little higher.

Longing is from God. But He also wants to fill that longing. And then He will send another . . . each one to move us on up a little higher! But He cannot send a new one until the old ones are filled. Why do we keep the same old longings year in and year out?

I believe it is because we have not begun *fully to participate* in the very life of Christ which is in us!

The remainder of this book I share with you from my own life and from the lives of persons whom I know intimately. I am merely witnessing.

No one could have been *less* indwelt by the life of Christ, nor less interested in being indwelt by the life of Christ than I was just a few years ago.

Then I received Him and He came in.

And as I have decreased, He has increased.

And as I have allowed Him to increase by taking my-

24

self out of His way (however slowly and stubbornly) I have found to my great joy and constant wonder that as I remember to participate in His life within me, *I am fulfilled.*

When He comes in, everything we long for comes in with Him.

Our part is to *take it.*

Even when it means inconvenience for us!

When it would be easier to say, "I'm afraid I'm not courageous enough to do this thing" . . . we *can take of* His courage and do it.

His courage is in us when He is in us.

". . . Paul . . . thanked God, and *took courage.*"

Paul *participated* in—shared the life of Christ within him. ". . . yet not I, but Christ liveth in me. . . ." The great Apostle had access to the very courage of Christ Himself. And he took it. In almost every instance, it *did* inconvenience Paul, humanly speaking. But it fulfilled his deepest longing at the same time because to Paul to live *was* this Jesus Christ Himself!

"O God, thou art my God; early will I seek thee: my soul thirsteth for thee, my flesh longeth for thee in a dry and thirsty land, where no water is."

"O God, thou art my God; early will I seek thee . . ."!

Longing is a gift of God for God Himself to fulfill. *With* Himself.

2. I DID *NOT* LONG FOR SALVATION!

I, personally, did not long for salvation.

I laughed at the word.

Many persons *do* long for it. Many others do not. I have heard Christians say: "I'm not wasting any more time with *him*. He's not interested in salvation!"

My heart has longed to run to the fellow, who is probably not one bit interested in the Christian's "salvation," and tell him about my Saviour!

Most unconverted adults in our portion of the twentieth century are a product of the humanistic materialism which flooded our schools and colleges during the twenties and thirties. They do not, as I did not, even know what salvation is!

And so don't care.

Or pretend not to.

But something within us all is strangely *attracted* to the Person of Jesus Christ. For years I contended that Jesus and Socrates were my two favorite characters in history.

Still I don't once remember having called someone of high character a *Socrates*-like person.

The loftiest compliment I could pay a man or a woman was to say, "There is a *Christ*-like person!"

Many do not believe He is the Son of God, the only Saviour of the human race, but something in His personality *attracts everyone*!

Even though Jesus declared that He and the Father were One, and even though a man may say this is *not* what he believes, still I have yet to find one who will commit himself by accusing Christ of lying or misrepresenting things.

The usual answer is . . . "Well, you have your interpretation and I have mine . . . et cetera, et cetera."

Something in us all *responds* to Him, because whether we believe it or not, He *is* God's revelation of Himself and we were created in the first place to belong to God.

To be one with Him.

The life union was broken. But once we experience the healing touch of Christ in our lives, we begin to feel more and more "at home" again.

The air of heaven was meant to be our native air.

If you call salvation a "way out" of your troubles, or think of it as a process whereby God becomes a heavenly "Yes-Man" to you, then you may long for salvation. Most persons don't think of it one way or another. This may shock the average Christian, but it is true.

Those of us who believe that God sets forth His plan

27

for salvation in the writings of the New Testament know that man simply needs to "believe on the Lord Jesus Christ" in order to be saved. Those of us who have tried it have seen that "belief" shifted *for* us by the Holy Spirit to something we *know*.

Something knowable only to the heart.

Those of us who have moved our central confidence from ourselves to the Person of Jesus Christ have begun to believe on Him and we know we are experiencing personal salvation. We can't explain it. Unless we're still counting upon the merits of our *own* wits and wisdom, we don't even try to explain it.

We receive it.

We enjoy it.

We experience it.

We use it.

Paul said to his Philippian jailer: ". . . Believe on the Lord Jesus Christ, and thou shalt be saved. . . ."

The jailer "believed" and he was saved. Changed. Transformed from a man who inflicted stripes to a man who washed them. From a man who locked other men in prison to a man who set them free and gave them of his own meat and bread.

The jailer *believed* on the Lord Jesus Christ and he was saved.

Jesus taught that those who do *not* believe are cut off from Him.

". . . ye believe not, because ye are not of my sheep.

28

. . . My sheep hear my voice, and I know them, and they follow me: And I give unto them eternal life; and they shall never perish, neither shall any man pluck them out of my hand."

If you do not believe on the Lord Jesus Christ as you read these lines, then you simply do not have eternal life. This is not my idea. It is God's plan. And God is not on trial. We are. We will either believe or we will not.

He won't force us.

Sometimes I wish He would. But He cannot because free will is also His idea. Not ours. Most of us would prefer *not* to choose. We do a lot of rebellious talking about our need of freedom. We bruise our hearts and our minds and our egos, battering at the wall of what *seems* to pen us in. But actually, most of us would prefer to have someone else make our choices for us.

Particularly in the choice of believing on the Lord Jesus Christ. And few are willing to face the indisputable fact that even when we do not choose *for* Him, we are still choosing—*against* Him.

"He that is not with me is against me. . . ."

Jesus Christ declares Himself to *be* life itself.

". . . I am the way, the truth, and the life. . . ."

". . . I am the resurrection, and the life: he that believeth in me, though he were dead, yet shall he live: And whosoever liveth and believeth in me shall never die . . ."!

". . . Believe on the Lord Jesus Christ, and thou shalt be saved. . . ."

To be saved is to have eternal life.

And if Jesus Christ *is* eternal life, then being saved is *having* Jesus Christ.

Salvation is what He does for us because He *is* the Saviour. And being human and most interested in ourselves, we tend to talk more about our salvation than we do about our Saviour!

But we can stop this.

We control our conscious minds and we can bring this off-center emphasis to a sudden stop right now. We can bow our heads before this Saviour and ask His forgiveness for making the theme of our Christian song the worth of the gift instead of the still greater worth of the giver. I pray every day for a more grateful heart . . . a heart that somehow learns to respond with thanksgiving for the unspeakable gift of my salvation. But mine is the kind of heart that wants to respond to a giver even above His gift.

Do I dare point you to my salvation?

Can you receive eternal life because I have received it?

No.

You can be convinced that eternal life is available to you by looking at my eternal life and believing that if this wonder is for such as I, it can be for such as you, too.

But my salvation cannot save you.

Only my Saviour can do that.

Not my salvation . . . my Saviour.

Not my salvation . . . my Saviour.

Look at my Saviour.

Look at *the* Saviour!

And find your own eternal life, "Looking unto Jesus the author and finisher . . ." of it all.

My paternal grandmother, whom I called Gram, had a native knack for using a tone of voice, just a touch above a whisper, to call me, as a child, into happily isolated, completely cozy moments alone with her as the two of us inspected a bird's nest or a new and nestling violet patch. Sometimes she would call me in this particular "Genie voice" to come and stand beside her at our kitchen door and "smell that good sweet air!" Still more delightful to me were the times she called me over her shoulder as she stooped beside a prize rose bush (which she more often than not called her "Genie rose"). And when I came tripping up beside her, all set for sharing two or three of those cozy moments, when no one else stood on the earth but my Gram and me, she would cup a long lovely rosebud in her hand reverently and say:

"Would ja' jist look at that? Would ja' jist *look*!"

My grandmother was not an educated woman. And she was not even proud of the fact that she could practically stick a pencil into the ground and make the pencil grow! She expected things to grow. She was simple enough and wise enough to revere the very *life* of that rose.

She was in awe of it.

In a deep and profound and marvelous way this simple woman and this simple child bowed before the *life* in that rose.

Gram wouldn't have thought of trying to describe the rose.

She knew perfectly well that it could speak for itself.

It was right there and she simply called me to look at it, and without a thought of analyzing her knowledge, she knew I would know what she meant when she said: "Would ja' jist look?"

Has anyone ever spoiled a sunset for you by attempting to describe it while standing right beside you as you look at the same sunset? Some things won't yield to description. Good writers don't even try. People with no reverence for the sunset or with an exaggerated notion of their own descriptive powers will always stand right there beside you and "describe" the view at which your very heart is *looking*!

My very heart and my brain—even my hands on the keys of this typewriter long to describe the Saviour to you.

But I know I cannot.

There is something I *can* do, however. I can call you into a close, complete moment with me as I share with you the ways in which He has become my everything.

For the next few pages will you come and look with me at Jesus Himself?

He is the One who is living in you, too, if you have received Him.

Will you just *look*—at *Him*?

3. I LONGED TO *LOOK* AT GOD!

A few minutes before I received Jesus Christ as my Saviour, I asked my friend who was helping me find my way . . . "What does God look like to you?"

Without taking time for one small thought, she replied: "He looks like Jesus Christ."

Jesus Christ.

". . . I, if I be lifted up . . . will draw. . . ."

He does.

He drew me. Perhaps He has drawn you. If not yet, He is seeking your attention. Seeking *you*.

I was not attracted to my friend's "salvation." I was attracted to her *Saviour*. Just minutes before I became His, I was longing to *look* at Him!

Then, the Holy Spirit lighted up His face and in the next moment, I was His and He was mine forever.

One of the great creative works of the Holy Spirit is to make us *sure*. Sure that we are sinners and sure that we need a Saviour!

Every native in every dark jungle knows the burden of a guilty conscience. It is inevitable that any one of them could miss it. ". . . all have sinned, and come short of the glory of God." Everyone in the world. Everyone who has ever been in the world.

And for that reason *everyone* needs a Saviour.

The jungle-man doesn't know why, perhaps, but something within him goads and drives him to try this and that sacrifice to this and that god in order to relieve himself of the heavy weight of guilt for his sins.

In this respect the native is more advanced than many members of so-called civilized society. In this respect the native is less neurotic. Neurotics don't see themselves as they are. Neurotics see themselves in the *images* which they themselves have conjured up. The jungle-man is clearer here.

He sees himself as needing to be relieved of sin.

He tries ineffectual methods, but he tries.

The so-called "Christian movements" which teach that we already contain within us all the "good" we need—that God approves of us as we are—that we only need somehow to "latch on" to this nebulous divine approval, contribute a great deal to the making of neurotics. God's estimate of us is in the Holy Bible and there He says, "There is *none* righteous, no, not one."

To say God approves of us is to hide behind our own neurotic image of ourselves and thereby refuse to be *changed* back into the image of God.

35

But, in spite of the swamp of teaching abroad today that we need only to develop the "good" that is already in us, one after another continues to "come out" of these cults and fall relieved at the feet of Jesus Christ to receive forgiveness!

The Holy Spirit *convicts* of sin.

The "groups" may teach "goodness." But the Holy Spirit will bring to our remembrance that which we *must* know in order to find victorious life under *all* circumstances, and this is that "all have sinned" and all need a Saviour.

A Saviour is One who touches us at the place we cannot reach.

Those of us who have been struck to our knees and caused by the Holy Spirit to cry out for forgiveness at the foot of the cross of Jesus Christ . . . those of us who have *seen* ourselves through His eyes, as God sees us . . . those of us who have been stopped short in our mad hurtling to eternal destruction by the merciful hand of the One who reaches toward all men . . . those of us who have stared in blank horror at the *fact* that we are living corpses until the life of God has been *put within* us, *know* beyond any doubt that because *that* life is holy it cannot—it simply *could not* be put within us as we are because we are sinful! *Until* our sin is forgiven by Jesus Christ.

He touches us and cleanses us in the depths we cannot reach.

Then, and only then, can He come into us to dwell in the Person of the Holy Spirit. Then and only then is there true *goodness* within us.

Jesus Christ had to *become* sin *for* us on the cross of Calvary and we have to receive Him *before* His righteousness *can* be put within us!

"For he hath made him to be sin for us, who knew no sin; that we might be made the righteousness of God in him."

He is our righteousness.

His righteousness comes right along with Him when He comes.

Any virtue or goodness we might have inherited or developed naturally *is* as "filthy rags" compared to the righteousness of God. Those of us who have experienced His righteousness being *put within* us at the time of our turning to Christ and those of us who have given this righteousness, this life, room to grow, *know* that the "filthy rags" simile is altogether true.

The contrast is breath-taking.

And so . . . when we face reality in both ourselves *and* in Christ we can do nothing but trust Him COMPLETELY for our salvation. We see that we cannot earn it. We cannot deserve it. We cannot achieve it. We cannot capture it. We cannot learn it. We cannot absorb it.

We can only *receive* the *gift* of God.

And the gift of God is Jesus Christ Himself.

He is our salvation. His very life which He puts within us at our "new birth" *is* the dynamic of our salvation. ". . . I will *put* a new spirit *within* you. . . . And I will put *my* spirit within you. . . ."

We trust Him for a special process called salvation . . . but *then* . . . (and this is why I have asked you to look with me at the Saviour Himself) . . . but *then,* once He has saved us, we begin to take things into our own hands!

We begin to *try* to grow.

We begin to *try* to increase our faith.

We begin to *try* to abide.

We begin to *try* to be peaceful.

And hour after hour, day after day, week after week, month after month, this Jesus Christ stands reminding us with the simplicity and majesty of God Himself that ". . . without me ye can do nothing"!

". . . without me ye can do nothing."

Why do we continue to try?

Is it because we think Christ Himself was confused about the reality of things when He said what He said to His disciples as it is recorded in the fifteenth chapter of the Gospel of John? Or is it because we feel we need to help Him accomplish that good work which He has begun in us? Do we think He is inadequate to one or two things which we feel we had better work out ourselves?

What is it?

Stop and think.

"Search me, O God, and . . . see if there be any wicked way in me . . ."!

Surely it is wicked to try to take God's place.

Surely it is wicked to doubt His power.

Surely it is wicked not to believe Jesus Christ meant what He said.

And He said quite clearly and with the simplest simplicity that *without Him* we can do absolutely nothing!

In utter, frantic helplessness at the sight of the sin in us when the Holy Spirit points it out, we turn to Christ for forgiveness. For salvation. And then . . . and then we take things into our own hands. Why?

Could it be ignorance on our part?

Could it be that we haven't been still before Him long enough to find out what He's really like?

Could it be that we haven't spent enough conscious time in His presence?

Could it be that we haven't fed our starving spirits on the Word of God?

Could it be that we haven't depended upon the Holy Spirit to open our understandings as we read what He inspired?

Could it be that we have missed the central point entirely?

Salvation *includes* growth, life, faith, abiding, prayer-life, peace, simplicity, as well as forgiveness of sin. And if the Saviour Himself *is* our salvation, wouldn't it be plausible to realize that in HIM *all things do* consist?

If salvation implies being saved, then looking unto the Lord Himself is the answer.

"Look unto *me,* and be ye saved. . . ."

"Come unto *me,* . . . and I will give you rest."

". . . *I* am the way, the truth, and the life. . . ."

My heart sings with joy because of that personal pronoun when it is used by Christ Himself. I'm so glad He's a person and not just a principle! I did not long for salvation. I longed for a Saviour.

"O God, thou art my God; early will I seek *thee* . . ."!

And now that our eyes are *upon* Jesus Christ the Person, we'll move on to see how it is that He *can* become all things to us. Even more to the point, we'll see how it is that He has already *become* all things to us and our part is to find out how we can begin to *experience* it. First we'll have a look at *growth.*

We all long to grow. Unless we are blind to our need.

Be prepared to feel pretty silly at your past efforts to add that "cubit" to your spiritual height.

I do.

4. I LONGED TO GROW!

Up to this point I have written to those who do and those who do not believe in Jesus Christ. In this chapter I will write primarily to those of you who not only believe in Him, but whose hearts long to follow Him as Lord of your lives.

This does not rule out non-believers or nominal Christians.

I believe that if you will read on (you who do not follow Christ with all your hearts) you will become jealous of what is in store for anyone who dares to follow Him the second half!

Again, I witness.

That happened to me. I became jealous of the freedom, the life, the perpetual upward motion in the lives of those whose gift of hinds' feet enabled them to leap and skip around the mountainside always in sight of Him, who was just up ahead. I grew jealous of their abandon, their gaiety, their joy, their ease in the rough places. Their growth.

Their fulfilled desires.

If you are yet undecided, please read on.

If you are stumbling on the way, please read on.

If you are singing on the way, please read on.

Longing springs from the heart of God.

He would give you a new and deeper longing for more of Himself.

I will write on.

Knowing, as I now do, that each new longing comes from the God who fulfills it.

The sincere Christian longs to grow.

It is as natural for the Christian to grow while he is looking at the *Son* as it is for the daisy to grow while it looks at the *sun*! Growth is natural when the conditions of growth are met. Growth does not exist of itself. It is the result of life.

Growth is not the result of itself.

It is the result of the presence of *life*.

And life does not come from the roots of a plant; it comes from beyond. From below the roots.

From God.

Life *is* within us, but it does not *come* from within us.

Life comes from God.

The life of the daisy and our life too.

There is a kind of life which the daisy cannot get, however, even from God. That is eternal life. Eternal life is for us only. Because only we are made in the image of God. And eternal life *is* God's life.

But following the already laid down natural laws of life, even eternal life does not come from within. *Especially* eternal life does not come from within.

It comes from *beyond.*

It comes from Christ. It *is* His very life.

It comes to invade us when we receive Him in His resurrection fullness. Then it is surely *within* us.

But *not* until we receive Him.

". . . if any man will open the door, I will come in. . . ." And *then* there will be *growth.* Because *He* is life. ". . . I am the resurrection, and the life. . . ."

Letters we receive leave us with varied feelings. One kind inevitably leaves me feeling—helpless. It is from the earnest soul who writes, "I don't seem to be growing in my Christian life. Tell me, please, what is the secret of your growth?"

I feel limp when I receive a letter like that.

And somewhat dismayed that someone should ask *me* when Jesus Christ Himself anticipated that question and answered it in the plainest of language!

"Which of you by taking thought can add one cubit to your stature?"

Do not jump to quick conclusions here. "Thought" is required to know what Jesus meant. Thought or plans or mental-gyrations will not make you grow one cubit, but thought is always required to know what Jesus means. Even after the Holy Spirit reveals it to us, we must weigh it with our enlightened intelligences. And what the Lord Jesus said in effect is that *effort on our part does not promote growth.*

He Himself is our growth!

Because He Himself is our life.

Where there is life, there will be growth, and there will continue to be growth as long as the conditions of life are met.

Growth is an all-inclusive, wonder-filled sense of love living!

Growth is love—*living*!

The Beloved Disciple John late in his life lifted his voice and declared that ". . . God is love."

Where God is, love is.

Where God is, life is.

Where life is, growth is.

And so growth is love living!

There are many signs of growth in the Christian. We will look at only two. First . . . am I honest with myself and with God?

Am I honest with myself and with God?

It is impossible to be one without the other. If I am not facing facts as they are (especially facts about myself) with *myself,* then I cannot be honest with God when I discuss myself and my problems with Him!

Of course, God knows this. But my will is the spring which releases His power to untangle me in the depths which I cannot reach and if I am misrepresenting the facts, even to myself, how can my will be an act of clear-cut decision on the *right* issues?

I listened, not long ago, for over an hour to a disturbed woman who poured out her longing to see her husband become a Christian. Her desire seemed right. On the surface, it was even scriptural. But after that hour, I managed to get in a word or two, and I asked a question which I knew could and probably would end the interview abruptly one way or another: "*Why* do you want your husband to become a Christian? Do you want him to do this because you see how much Jesus Christ needs a man with his capabilities and personality? Or do you want him to become a Christian so that *you* can be proven right?"

Her quick flush and sharp answer showed me that her motives were definitely *mixed*. She was not being honest with herself and, of course, God could not answer her prayers.

In my own experience I have found over and over that I have prayed vainly for a Christian brother or sister who seemed to need an enormous amount of changing. At first, my prayers consisted of a long complaint to God (sometimes in the King James Version, sometimes not), *about* this brother or sister. Usually the complaint reminded God with regular frequency how Christ-like *I* was acting in the situation and that if God didn't change this one who offended *soon*, I'd surely have to take some steps to help Him in the correction!

After months of this, God finally got through to me with: "If you see sin in that life, it's only because I have given you the perception. Your part is to double your own efforts to protect My reputation with those involved who do not know Me."

In one case in particular, I obeyed on this point.

That was one sign of growth.

But still God could not answer the prayer completely. This brother was still hard at it and everywhere I turned I seemed to run into more of the results of his flaming ego at work among a certain group of non-believers with whom I had been quite proud of my own Christian witness.

This brother was *not* behaving like Jesus Christ.

Not at all.

But I could almost *feel* myself grow when once more God got me quiet long enough to realize that my motives were not altogether unmixed! I was not being completely honest with myself.

Praying for this brother to change was right.

But *using* his un-Christian behavior to point up my own Christian behavior was not right.

I had been doing this and was not willing to admit it to myself.

And certainly I wasn't admitting it to God!

But, of course, God knew it anyway.

Are we really honest with ourselves?

Are our motives mixed or unmixed?

46

If we are honest with ourselves, we are honest with God.

And if we are honest with both ourselves and God, we can relax and *know* we are growing up in Jesus Christ.

Jesus Christ always faces facts as they are. He did not always answer the surface questions which were put to Him when He was on earth, but He *did* always answer the *real* questions which lay squirming beneath the ones formed into words.

He *is* my honesty if I permit Him full sway in my life.

Christ in me is my *only* hope of—honesty!

With God and with myself.

And if I am honest with myself about myself, I am growing.

He is always honest.

He is my growth.

Anyone can grow. No one has a corner on the market of spiritual growth. Once the life of God has been put within us at the moment we receive Jesus Christ as our Saviour, growth *can* begin.

He wants to be your Saviour and He also wants to be your growth.

He can be because He *is* your life if you have received Him.

One more among many signs of spiritual growth (almost too obvious to mention!) is *maturity*. When we grow, we grow—*up*. We grow to maturity, don't we? Or at least we are supposed to be growing *toward* it. But how many of us confuse Christian *busyness* with maturity? How many of us confuse noisy meetings and numbers of forced testimonies with true spiritual maturity? Noisy meetings *can* be meetings of mature Christians. And certainly many busy Christians are mature, or at least maturing. The point I want to make is simply that the common signs we use are not always accurate.

Mature Christians are Christians who *act* more and more every day like Jesus Christ.

Some of the most immature Christians I know read their Bibles every day and many of them can recite pages of Scripture from memory. But in the tight places they ridicule and criticize and blaze away in judgment and condemnation of other Christians who might not interpret those well-memorized Scripture verses just as *they* do and nowhere in their behavior or personalities can we find any family resemblance to the Saviour.

Or any evident signs of true maturity.

To me, the most evident sign of true maturity is the ability to adjust.

How quickly do you adjust?

How quickly do I adjust?

When you've planned for a quiet afternoon alone and an alcoholic for whom you've been praying rings your doorbell—how quickly do you adjust?

When I've set aside a long-cherished evening to digest a new book on "the deeper life," what do I do when a dear soul who has been praying for me for years "just thought she'd drop by for an hour or so between trains to bring me a tin of cookies and chat awhile"?

How quickly do I adjust?

Especially when I'm dieting and can't eat the cookies!

If the contractor promises moving day in plenty of time to get settled before Thanksgiving and you find yourself not only trying to prepare Thanksgiving dinner amidst packing crates, but see no hope of putting up the Christmas tree in your new home—how quickly do you adjust?

In my B.C. days, and during a good part of my early Christian life, I excelled at maladjustment. If something didn't go to please me, I felt I had a right to let off some steam about it!

At least I had a right to make the other person uncomfortable too.

But that was before I woke up to the blessed, glad truth that *only* as I give up the *rights* to myself along with my SELF, am I free!

I had read about rejoicing in *all* things.

But somehow it had to do with St. Paul, not with me.

And then slowly I began to see that I would be mature only when Jesus Christ was living His life *fully* in me. I would be mature *only* when once and for all, I took Galatians 2:20 as the standard for my personal, everyday life.

"I am crucified with Christ: nevertheless I live; yet not I, but Christ liveth in me. . . ."

I, as I, am not mature!

But "I am crucified with Christ." Still I am living and moving about this earth in a mortal body, ". . . yet not, I but *Christ liveth in me* . . ."!

I, as I, could not adjust quickly.

I, as I, did not even want to.

"Nevertheless not I—but Christ" who *does* want to!

And since the moment I took Galatians 2:20 as the standard for my hourly living, He has given me chance after chance to try it.

One fine opportunity came several months ago when I finished a week's speaking engagement on a Sunday morning in Portland, Oregon, and was scheduled to fly to Seattle, Washington, in time to speak at the evening service in a Seattle church.

The week in Portland had been one of those weeks which look comfortably full on Monday and end up "pressed down and running over" as I staggered "pressed down" physically toward its close. I was exhausted and I had a virus. How I longed to take a plane back to Chicago and my own bed!

Instead, I began my next engagement with a two-hour wait in the Portland airport and when my plane could not take off due to engine trouble, I was put on another plane whose pressurization apparatus was not working quite right.

I am a good flyer, as long as the pressurization apparatus *is* working. But that day, I sat huddled in a cramped, overheated coach plane, swallowing madly in a futile effort to unstop my ears . . . unable to convince the woman next to me that I had all but lost my voice from too much speaking the week before . . . coughing, massaging my aching head and neck, trying to comfort myself with the reassuring thought that I'd soon be on the ground in Seattle and bathed and resting in my friend Sylvia Hatfield's comfortable apartment.

"Things could be a lot worse," I told myself. "You could be hungry and you could be landing just in time for the evening service so you'd have to speak in this horribly wrinkled suit. You could even have a radio or a TV interview this very afternoon. But you don't. So things could be a lot worse."

Determinedly I put my *will* into thanking the Lord for the whole thing. I didn't *feel* thankful, but I thanked Him anyway. Although I allowed myself the luxury of thinking how sorry Mother would be for me if she could see her darling daughter sitting there courageously thanking God while the growing pressure pain in her head and ears forced tears to trickle down her cheeks!

By the time the plane landed, I was almost deaf and the pain had moved down to include both shoulders and my arms. "It could be worse though. After all, your ears will open up and you are going straight to Sylvia's apartment and then you can bathe and rest and change into fresh clothes. Plenty of time before your next appearance for at least an hour's sleep."

51

As I trudged down the steps from the plane to the ground I saw Sylvia waving frantically from the airport gate. I wondered why she was so eager to see me and as I came nearer, my ears popped enough so I heard her shout: "Hurry, Genie, hurry! We have just twenty minutes to make a radio interview and it takes almost that long to drive to the station from here!"

Now, I had rather looked forward to losing my luggage as a Christian. You see, I'd lost it a couple of times in my old life and each time I blistered the ears of any hapless rail or airline employee in sight. Both times I was completely convinced the railroad or airline had held a special board meeting at which detailed plans were laid to lose *my* luggage! The entire railroad and airline operations had been "out to get" Eugenia Price.

And so I wondered how I would react and what I would do as a Christian under the same circumstances.

That day I found out.

As Sylvia propelled me along toward the luggage counter, I "surrendered" having to make an appearance at a radio station in my wrinkled suit, but thanked God I could have a freshly pressed one from my luggage for the evening service.

And then the big chance came.

"Miss Price, I'm so sorry to have to tell you this, but your luggage was left in Portland by mistake."

With my head still spinning with pain, I wondered vaguely why the poor airline chap felt he needed to add "by mistake," but beyond that I just stood there surprised at the sudden wave of compassion for the young man which swept over me!

And yet, there it was. Unmistakably I felt sorry for him as he stood there adjusting his tie and straightening his trim cap preparatory to giving me "apology number 1-A for ruffled passengers whose luggage has just been left behind in Portland"—by mistake.

He opened his mouth to begin, but I said: "Better save your speech for someone else who needs it. I'm a Christian and I've *never* been more delighted to be one than I am right this minute. And you may not know it, but *you* should be glad I'm a Christian too!"

The fellow couldn't answer me, so I went on as Sylvia and I both began to laugh. "I'm dog-tired from the week I just finished and more thankful than I could ever tell you that I don't have to waste any more energy being sorry for myself or cutting you down to size. It's all right. The Lord knows where my luggage is and when you find it, please send it in a taxi to this address."

Did *I* make that adjustment?

No.

Jesus Christ made it *in* me.

". . . yet not I, but Christ liveth in me. . . ."

The interview at the radio station had a fresh ring to it too, *not* because I was especially original (*I* was especially *un*original!) but it was not I, but Christ who *gave* me the fresh proof that I *was* growing up.

53

I can be mature because Christ Himself is mature.
Jesus Christ *in* me, my *only* hope of maturity!

I became a Christian when I was physically thirty-three years old. At thirty-three years of physical age, I was an immature "sixteen" emotionally . . . still frantically trying to prove *my* point in everything.

Now? . . . Jesus Christ *in* me, my *only* hope of maturity.

Christ *in* me, my only hope of—growth!

5. I LONGED TO BELIEVE

The most difficult thing about becoming a Christian as an adult is to begin to believe. And yet the only qualification for becoming a Christian is to begin "to believe on the Lord Jesus Christ."

When we do that, He comes in.

But at first I couldn't believe.

All the arguments about *why* I should believe, only seemed to make it more impossible. I was trying to do it with my mind. I listened to the reasons why I should believe and I listened and digested them with my mind and then went right on trying to take the step also with my mind.

We take the step with our *will*.

Our will empowered by the Holy Spirit. Unless He gives us the power to place our wills in the hands of Jesus Christ, we can't do it. I believe we definitely have the choice to make. Some will disagree with me. But while I do believe God continues to respect our free will, we are powerless to turn that will toward *God* without the work of the Holy Spirit! We can choose to turn toward our selfish selves alone. But not toward God. I believe it is a two-way transaction, with our part entirely dependent upon His grace poured out in His mercy and His love and His caring about us. He showed the extent of all of that caring on the cross, so we can depend upon it that He will stand ready to give that power wherever we will make our choice to *take* the power.

I am inclined to think that down deep enough or up high enough there is a point of agreement here among all Christians who differ so widely and sometimes violently on the terminology used.

Personally, I know I was *given* the very ability to turn to Christ in that hotel room in New York City in the month of October, 1949. A decision like that was totally unlike me, as I was that day *before* Christ came to live within me.

And so, one of the first longings set astir within me when He began to press in upon my heart was the longing to *believe*.

I longed to believe.

First I simply longed to believe *something*.

Anything.

I was lost.

I couldn't admit it, but I had never really had a "way" that was clear cut. One I could see and follow.

I needed a way to live and I knew it and I longed to believe in something beyond myself.

But it was not until it was *revealed* to me, from *outside* myself, by way of my longing *heart,* that Jesus Christ and God *are* one and the same, that I began to be able to believe that He could give me a new life.

When at last my eyes were opened to see that God's every intention toward me was *in* this Jesus Christ, I believed.

". . . I, if I be lifted up . . . will draw. . . ."

He did. He drew me, gave me the very ability to open my heart to Him, and then He came in.

As every other Christian, I trusted the Person of Jesus Christ to make this eternal transaction in me.

And then, as with almost every other Christian, I began to long again. As they, I also longed for faith and more faith. And although I trusted Him for my salvation, I began to try to whip up *faith* myself!

It is said that the devil flees from the sight of a Christian on his knees. I am inclined to doubt this. Certainly the devil has gotten in some of his best licks with me while I have been on my knees! On my knees working feverishly to conjure up a *mental attitude* which I could recognize as *faith.* On my knees in an attitude of tense striving to whip up in my imagination a picture of the thing for which I prayed—as *I* thought it *should* be. On my knees with set jaw and clenched fists explaining anxiously and in detail to God just how He can go about helping me out of the difficulty . . . or how He can use this device and that method to change the person or persons whose disposition clashes are making trouble for me.

On my knees "manufacturing" faith.

And the devil is having the time of his evil life!

Making full use of my futile self-effort.

But I hang my head in shame that during so much of the time I have spent in such a manner on my knees, only God and the devil seemed to know about the futility angle!

I was slow to learn.

Then some months ago a certain tragic situation arose which involved persons who are very, very dear to me. My heart ached constantly. I set a regular prayer time each day about which I told no one. I kept it religiously. Every day at the appointed hour I was on my knees— fists clenched, eyes wet with tears, jaw set, mind working, *working* to "whip up" the attitude of faith. Long and detailed instructions poured forth to the Father in heaven in the name of the Son. I imagined the persons involved smiling at each other again . . . arms around the neck . . . heart to heart as Christians are supposed to be, according to the Scriptures.

Regularly I prayed and wept and pleaded and conjured up "faith" and outlined procedures to God and— nothing whatever happened.

Then one day I was exhausted. I just knelt there

drooping and said, "Lord, I can't think of anything else to say!"

And He said: "Good."

Then He took over. With simple, swift strokes the Holy Spirit seemed to be drawing a picture which even I could interpret. No words came, but suddenly I *knew* that I had no faith outside of Christ Himself. Suddenly I realized that He Himself is my faith too!

Within a few months there was the miracle of another answered prayer.

". . . the life which I now live in the flesh I live *by the faith of the Son of God. . . .*"

Would Jesus Christ come to indwell me in the Person of the Holy Spirit and leave His faith in heaven?

No!

The thought stabbed me into awareness that here was a deeper rest about which I had not yet heard. He is my *faith* too. I could from that time on pray in the name of Jesus Christ and *in His faith*. The very same faith that gave Him the courage to commend His Spirit into His Father's hands as He hung as a man on the cross of Calvary.

The same faith that overcame that same Satan when he tried to put suggestions of self-effort into the Lord's mind in the wilderness, just as he had tried to put them into my mind as I too knelt in prayer. The same Lord who turned Satan down flatly in the wilderness was right there to turn him down for me too.

And He did.

In no uncertain terms.

I didn't even try to pray any more about the tragic situation. I did try to thank Him and then got up and went about my work as though for the first time, the fact of His presence and His intense interest in the same situation had just penetrated my dense mind! Of course He was with the persons involved in my "tragic situation." Of course He loved them more than I did. Of course He wanted the whole thing straightened out too. Even more than I did. His stakes in it were much higher than mine.

Of course He didn't need me to tell Him how to handle it.

Of course He had faith in Himself. *Of* Himself.

Of course He brought that faith along when He came to live in me.

Of course He Himself *is* my faith!

What a relief. What a rest. What a leap forward.

And then it began to clear up still more for me. The two blind men who heard that Jesus was passing by outside of Jericho, did not cry out—"Thou son of David, we have conjured up great faith and are declaring that we can see again!"

No.

They cried—". . . Have mercy on us, O Lord, thou son of David"!

And Jesus stopped and looked at them.

But He did not say, "Because I see that you have done a splendid piece of work whipping up your faith, I will help you."

He just looked at them and said, ". . . What will ye that I shall do unto you?"

"What will ye that *I* shall do unto you?"

What do you want *Me* to do for you?

He Himself was their faith.

And that faith made them whole.

Faith is having confidence in God. Naturally, we cannot have faith in someone whom we do not know. So, the more we know God, the more confidence we have in Him. But who knows God better than God Himself? And why would not God's faith be the ultimate?

It would be.

It is!

Jesus Christ Himself is our faith. "In whom we have boldness and access with *confidence by the faith of him.*"

Growth is love—living.

Faith is love—*confiding.*

God is love.

God has supreme confidence in Himself.

He declared Himself in Jesus Christ . . . "In whom we have boldness and access with confidence by the faith *of him.*"

Therefore true faith is love confiding.

We can relax and draw on the riches in glory by the *faith* of Christ Jesus Himself. *If* . . . *if* we *know* that

61

"the life which (we) now live in the flesh (we) live by the faith of the Son of God, who loved (us) and gave himself for (us)."

I longed to believe . . . I longed to have faith.

From now on I can pray with His faith.

What a relief to know that He *Himself* is my faith!

6. I LONGED TO BE CONSTANT

Christ *in* me . . . my only hope of *growth*.
Christ *in* me . . . my only hope of *faith*.
He is my growth. He is my faith.
And He Himself is my very *abiding*! My constancy.
How is this so? Perhaps you think, "I can comprehend what is meant by saying He is my growth. I can see this because Jesus Christ Himself tells me that He is 'the resurrection and the *life*.' That He Himself is 'the way, the truth, and the *life*.' And so, since I know *growth* is a natural result of *life*, and since I have His Own Word for it that He Himself comes in to be my very *life* when I receive Him, then I can comprehend that He is my growth. Since the Word of God also tells me that 'the life which I now live in the flesh I live by the faith *of* the Son of God . . . ,' I can understand that he is also my *faith*."

"I have God's Own Word for *growth* and *faith*."

"But how is it that Jesus Christ Himself can be my constancy, my *abiding*?"

"Does He not tell me that *I* am to abide in *Him*?"

Yes, He does tell you that. He tells me that too. And every Christian believer who hungers for the deeper things of God *longs* to know a constant abiding in Jesus Christ. This is natural *after* we have been invaded by the *super*natural. The Holy Spirit coming in to dwell in us creates this longing for constancy to Jesus Christ. This is His Work . . . to make us long for unbroken communion with the Lord Jesus.

What sincere Christian, longing for more and more of Christ, does not promise God every morning that in this day he *will* abide?

"Oh, God, today I will . . . I *will* abide! I will remember that You live within me. I will remember that everywhere I go I have the reputation of the Son of God in my hands! I *will* remember to let You do the reacting through me every minute of this day!"

"Abide in me. . . ."

"Yes, Lord . . . I will abide in You."

This tender exchange takes place in our morning quiet time and by ten A.M. *that* person calls on the telephone or the washing machine breaks down and . . . ?

What happened to all that "abiding"?

Didn't we mean it when we promised the Lord just two short hours ago? It seemed such a logical, practical, simple thing to do. Sitting in our "chair of heavenly bliss" as we meditated upon God's Words to us, we thought ourselves rather silly not to have seen before

64

now that *striving* is the hard way! Today we would truly *abide*!

And then the washing machine broke down.

And so did the abiding!

The automobile stopped in heavy traffic.

And so did the abiding!

Why?

Didn't we promise? Yes. We promised.

Didn't we realize the seriousness of a promise to the Creator God? Yes. We realized the seriousness of such a promise.

Then why did we stop abiding?

Why?

I read everything I could find on the subject of abiding for over two years. I read and reread the fifteenth chapter of the Gospel of John. "I am the vine, ye are the branches. . . ."

Through and through my heart and mind came His voice asking me . . . commanding me . . . "Abide in me . . . without me ye can do nothing."

"The voice of my beloved."

I agreed with Him.

What a relief it was the day I discovered that without Him I *could* do absolutely nothing.

I agreed with Him that I should, that I *must* abide in Him.

I truly wanted to.

And yet . . . those times kept coming. Although He

always forgave me and restored me to the closeness with Himself we knew before I broke my promise to abide, I grew sick of the failures and I cried out to Him one day to teach me the secret of abiding in a way even I could understand!

He did.

And this is the story of that lesson.

At thirty-seven years of age I remained a spoiled brat in one big respect at least. Even though I had been a Christian for four years, my parents were still buying most of my clothes. This had been a way in which we had "spoiled" each other in the years past. Naturally I cut down on the quantity after my conversion, but the time came when I faced the fact that I must not only begin to buy my own clothes, what was worse (to me), I must begin to shop for them myself!

This was the part I resisted most.

For years I had made fun of people who attended sales. My things were selected for me by Mother and the faithful saleswomen in an exclusive store in my home town where they loved me (or tried to) in spite of my unpleasant arrogance everytime I had to "bother" to try on something.

They were accustomed to me.

I suspect they realized some of my fussiness was due to my self-consciousness at wearing such large sizes and went on placating me through the years because Mother was such a dear friend and good customer.

This haughty attitude on my part was *not* like Jesus Christ.

I had known it for sometime. Finally I informed Ellen (the friend who led me to Christ and who is now my associate) that I was ready to launch out on a shopping trip—*and* at the after-Christmas sale season!

She gasped quietly and said: "All right. I'll go with you. But let's have a prayer first—and *you* pray."

I prayed.

A very spiritual prayer, I thought. I told God I knew He knew my needs and that I was sure He had just the two suits I needed at just the prices I could pay and I promised Him frequently throughout the prayer that I *would* abide in Him every minute of the entire shopping expedition!

The first sales lady we approached had obviously *lost* all her Christmas spirit. I smiled at her (proud that for the first time in years I had lost enough weight to wear an eighteen right off the rack!) and said: "Could I see some eighteens, please?"

Her *look,* which swept right down over the end of her patrician nose, said: "Sorry, Madam, we don't carry circus tents in this department!"

What she actually said was: "Sorry, we don't have anything that *large!*"

She intended to wither me. What she did was bring a mighty resurgence of the old Gene Price with all her soap opera dialogue banners flying! My great "spirituality" following my prayer was fractured as a razor-reply tore through my "abiding" mind and hung there teeming to be put into words.

In my old life I would have relished every moment of my "reply." I would have re-told the incident over and over, improving my "reply" with each telling. *Naturally,* I responded with every atom of Eve in me to such an exchange. It was my forte. I thoroughly enjoyed cutting people down to *my* estimate of their true size.

Naturally, this was true of the old Gene Price.

*Super*naturally, something new had happened!

I said nothing to her for a moment. And by pure self effort I held the "reply" I longed to make. *But* I could *not* hold back my "look." I returned hers intensified. I even cocked my eyebrow as I hadn't done in almost four years (a bit of business which I always felt increased the venom in any "look"), and said, with ice breaking from every word: "I'm terribly sorry to have disturbed you."

And walked away.

Ellen followed me in silence.

Outside on the street I could stand it no longer. My heart was broken at what I had done!

That woman had every right to wither me if she wanted to. I, as a disciple of Jesus Christ had *no* right whatever to return even her *look*! As I stood there on the sidewalk with Chicago's Loop pushing past me I wanted to cry. The only reason I hadn't exchanged

68

more words with her was because I was afraid she might recognize me as the author of a Christian radio program I was writing at that time, which originated in Chicago.

The only reason I said as little as I said was pure spiritual *pride*!

What had happened to my *abiding*?

Hadn't I promised the Lord just one minute before I stepped out of the door of our house that I would abide in Him?

My shame was intense.

My heartache more intense.

I was irritated with Ellen when she suggested maybe we should go home and try it another day.

Then notions of doing this crossed frantic desires to run back and find the saleswoman and apologize! All I could do was stand there in the noise and the crowd and try not to cry.

And then . . . the lesson came. Quietly, over the noise of Chicago's Loop. And at the first convenient stopping place I grabbed my New Testament from my purse and began to read the first sentence of John 15:4 over and over and over!

"Abide in me, and I in you."

"Abide in me, *and I in you.*"

"Abide in me, *AND I IN YOU.*"

Sitting on a stool at a glove counter in a big Loop department store, He taught me the lesson I had prayed to learn.

I had been trying *of my own self to abide in Him*!

Jesus Christ would not have *dared* command me to abide in Him if He had not fully intended to be abiding in me even during the time in which I did *not* abide in Him!

We stop with the first half of that sentence: "Abide in me."

His whole sentence reads: "Abide in me, and *I in you*."

You abide in me, and I'll be abiding in you.

If He had *not* been abiding in me, I would not have experienced my heartbreaking need outside that store. Without Him I would have enjoyed the incident as in my old life. Where Jesus Christ *is* sin is abashed! Sin is abashed and dumbfounded in His presence! In Saint John's first letter he tells us that "No one who is born of God makes a practice of sinning, because the . . . life-principle continues to live in him . . ." (Williams Translation). We cannot *practice* sinning because He is always, every minute *abiding in us*! He can trust Himself. He knows what He will do.

Abide in me, and *I will be abiding in you*!

This is the way I learned the lesson that "abiding" does not come in a separate package of my own making.

He Himself *is* my abiding!

7. TO BE PEACEFUL

Men gather around big polished tables and argue about how to make and keep peace in the world.

Magazines and books are filled with theories about peace.

Christianity is called "the gospel of peace." But Christianity has been in the world for almost two thousand years. And the world is still sitting on an atomic "powder keg"!

America is called a Christian country and one group of citizens of one color still throw rocks through the windows of the homes of another group of citizens because their skin is yet another color.

Every year billions of dazzling greeting cards go out across the world which read: "Peace on earth."

Every year murders increase and divorce rates increase and a new war, either hot or cold, springs up from somewhere.

71

Peace?

It gives one a vaguely uneasy feeling to think of the horror smeared across the bloody face of the world because of the shortage of peace. It gives one a far less vague case of jitters to think those atomic mushrooms *could* "grow" in our own front yard because there is no real peace in the world. One can almost hear the silent breaking of hearts across our world on the days when we "honor our war dead." Cemeteries are quiet places and the hearts of those who kneel beside the little cross-marked tombs break again each year silently because cemeteries are silent places and there is no answer anywhere to the world's heart-cry for peace.

No answer to the individual heart-cries for peace.

No answer anywhere in the world in anything.

Not for you and not for me.

Why?

Because we are seeking peace in the wrong places. By wrong methods. We have misunderstood, or purposely twisted what the angels said when the Prince of peace was born that first Christmas. We are expecting peace to come from some nebulous turn of events. We act as though the angels *prophesied* peace that other silent night.

As though they prophesied something yet to come at one crashing, silver moment.

The angels did not prophesy peace at all.

They *proclaimed* it!

72

They proclaimed that peace itself lay in that manger and would hang on a cross and then walk bodily out of a tomb, and save the people from their sins. Peace only comes to the world when the people in that world are peaceful people. And peace only comes to a people when they are rightly related to the Father by faith in His Son, Jesus Christ.

Peace comes in when Christ comes in.

Most books that offer a way of peace are popular.

Most peace conferences make the headlines.

Vacation spots where "peace grows *in you* as the green grass grows upon our greening hillsides" pour out their "peacefully" written literature.

Weary, harried men and women are urged to "come out to the old ball park and enjoy a peaceful afternoon away from your troubles."

Lots sell well in the suburbs because it's "peaceful in the country."

Books about the "religion of peace" contained in right thinking pile up and vanish from the bookstalls and men and women leave the "peace" of their new lots in the country for work each day in the hectic unpeace of the city. The books on peace pile up and vanish and the "peaceful" fans leave the "old ball park" and go home to the battle of the bulge in friend wife's ego because supper got cold when the game ran into extra innings. The books on peace pile up and vanish and the hot wars and the cold wars continue to break out and the quiet hearts break again beside the quiet graves in the cross-marked cemeteries.

"Where is God in all this?" cries the grief-torn woman whose husband died of shock because their two boys were murdered in cold blood by other human beings gone diabolically mad in this same civilized world whose bookstalls are piled high with books on peace!

"Where is God in all my suffering? And why should *I* be the one who has the kind of cancer no one can cure or even cut out?" A once pretty woman of thirty-eight buries her head in her pillow and tries to choke off the sobs of rebellion against the tragedy that turned her "peaceful" life into one of fear and dread and pain and certain death!

Someone brought this woman a book about how to be peaceful by teaching herself to think right thoughts and she threw it across the room and swore for the first time in her entire life! She had thought she was peaceful once. But her peace didn't hold.

True story after true story of speeded-up desperation under the heavens and the earth gone mad in its search for peace. Books about peace pile up and vanish from the bookstalls, and God calls down from His heaven saying: ". . . they have healed the hurt of . . . my people slightly, saying, Peace, peace; when there *is* no peace!"

There *is* no man-made peace that holds when the

ghastly circumstances of life pass our understanding! Man-made peace . . . peace in the peaceful bookstalls among the books about peace only heals the hurt slightly and men and women go on saying "Peace, peace . . . when there *is* no peace!"

"Peace on earth?" Is it possible?

Yes.

". . . peace through the blood of his cross. . . ." Peace *only* by the One who Himself said just before they killed Him: "Peace I leave with you, my peace I give unto you . . ." ". . . if it were not so, I would have told you. . . ."

Jesus Christ was not prophesying peace at random.

He spoke those tender, strong words to *His Own* disciples. He was on His way to the cross to die for every man and woman and child in the world. To open the way for everyone, with no exceptions, to know personally the "peace . . . which passeth all understanding. . . ."

He gives His peace now to *all* who are His Own. And He *wants* us all to be His Own. But because peace only comes through union with God, peace cannot exist where sin is. He is a Holy God.

Sin must be wiped out before the Holy One comes in.

Perhaps that is one reason He said what He said about leaving His peace, just before He went willingly to the cross to shed His Own blood that our sins might be

75

washed away. He made the promise of peace and then went about making the way for us to receive it.

Peace is not a separate thing.

We make the mistake of searching for it as though it is.

It is not.

Peace is a result of an unbroken communion with God, which includes unbroken communion with our fellow man as well. This is only possible when we are out of the way and Christ is living His Own peace-filled life in us.

We are not peaceful by nature.

Sin has invaded our nature as God made it in the beginning and sin is not a peaceful thing.

Peace is not something the Lord left for us in a package.

Peace cannot be put into a package or a book.

Paul sang it out as he saw it in the heart that broke on Calvary for *him*, when he wrote: ". . . now in Christ Jesus ye who sometimes were far off are made nigh by the blood of Christ. For *he is our peace. . . .*"

He is our peace!

Jesus Christ Himself is our peace!

Where He is, sin is abashed. Worry, anxiety, fear, self-pity, murder, rebellion at life . . . rebellion at God Himself which shows itself in alcoholism, neuroticism, skepticism, atheism, communism, or criticism, curls up and vanishes in the presence of the One who went to the cross and let His Own sinless heart break wide open under the horror-filled burden of *our* sin!

We cannot *think* our way to peace.

We can only know peace when we allow Him to do away with all the enemies of peace. And when we begin fully to ". . . walk in the light as he is in the light . . . ," his blood will *keep us cleansed*, minute by minute of the sin of even understandable self-pity!

The woman dying of cancer at thirty-eight and the woman whose husband died from the shock of his sons' murders have a perfectly understandable *human* right to pity themselves.

To cry out, "Why?"

But that very rebellion and self-pity robs them of the peace He left for them. If it were not so, He would have told us.

His peace does not come in packages. Nor does it come *only* to those who have walked with Him over a long period of years. Peace comes at once to the newly converted sinner who has felt the weight roll away. He doesn't know where it went. He may not know the front from the back of the Bible. I didn't. But I knew a peace I didn't even think existed when Jesus Christ forgave me of my sins.

Before my conversion, I had sung lustily at so-called sophisticated parties of this very thing. An amazing number of "pagans" know the lyrics to the old gospel songs. Over and over I led out with:

At the Cross, at the Cross, where I first
  saw the light,
And the burden of my heart rolled away,
It was there by faith, I received my sight,
And now I am happy all the day.

I sang it and laughed with everyone else and hours later, as I lay wide-eyed on my pillow trying to get the somewhat stilted melody out of my reeling mind, the tears on that pillow seemed more ridiculous than the song as the lyrics of the last line kept circling around in my brain . . .

And now I am happy all the day.

I tried many "peaceful" pastimes. Sometimes I felt peaceful. I had a splendid classical record collection at a certain period. Bach and Handel and Haydn and some of Beethoven made me feel peaceful.

I owned some "peaceful" books with fine old leather bindings.

But mostly my peaceful pursuits only made me long for peace.

The peace I now *know* in Jesus Christ.

The peace He said He'd leave with me.

The peace that came when He came. His peace. What kind of God would He be to come to live within me, according to His promise, and leave His peace in heaven?

Peace does not come in packages or by methods or in books. It is *in* Christ Jesus. And it is not reserved for those who have known Him a long time at all. A few months after my life story, *The Burden Is Light,* was reviewed in the Chicago *Tribune* Book Section, a letter came from Claude M., a prisoner at Joliet Penitentiary, saying that Mr. Lawrence Heron's arrestingly written review had attracted his attention.

"Where may I purchase this book? If it *is* 'for the scoffer,' as Mr. Heron claims, then I want to read it."

Sometime later we tied up this man's story with the front pages of every Chicago newspaper! Claude M. was a famous member of the underworld who had turned state's evidence at the time he wrote his letter of inquiry about my book. Through letters, prayers, a radio program I was writing, and a visit with him at Joliet Prison, this "big-time policy racket" boy became a son of God.

As we sat facing him across the visitors' barrier desk at the prison, we discovered that he had truly surrendered *his* life into the hands of Jesus Christ as he read through the pages of *my* life in *The Burden Is Light.*

There was no mistaking it.

He was a very newborn babe in Christ, but the life of Christ was *in* him and we relaxed in the presence of our new brother. He and I had both longed for the wrong things. I remember his smile when I said: "You didn't need a Saviour any more than I did. And I didn't need one any more than you did. The ground *is* level at the foot of the cross of Jesus Christ."

His smile was good and direct and redeemed.

His face was peaceful.

Because *Claude* was peaceful.

A man who is imprisoned for protection from the quick guns of the underworld is—peaceful? A man who, according to the federal office conducting the investigation, is in grave physical danger every minute he is outside the walls of the prison? This man is peaceful?

Yes.

In a letter received from my new brother in Christ only today he writes: "No one here can understand my seeming indifference to the drastic situation ahead of me. But how can they possibly know about my peace when they do not understand about our Saviour? I have belonged to Him such a short time, but I have found out in a way better than a hundred sermons, that He *is* my peace!"

Peace is *holding* this man.

When he leaves prison, nothing of this world is sure.

Claude M. may or may not read this book. But ". . . underneath are the everlasting arms. . . ."

The Saviour who is this prisoner's peace is also his eternal life.

The gang guns may blaze, but no one can kill my brother in Christ. The One who is *in* him, *is* life.

". . . I am the resurrection, and the life: he that believeth in me, though he were dead, yet shall he live:

80

And whosoever liveth and believeth in me shall *never* die. . . ."

It pleased the Father that in Jesus Christ should all fullness dwell.

"All fullness" includes Claude's peace and yours and mine.

Nothing can shake that peace because nothing changes Jesus Christ.

And He is our peace.

8. TO BE SENSITIVE

Jesus Christ is our "look" at God Himself.
　He is our salvation.
　He is our life, therefore, our growth.
　He Himself is our ability to believe. He is our faith.
　He Himself is our constancy. Our abiding.
　And He is our peace.
　He is all these for which we long and more. Because
we all long for more than these. Each one, however im-
portant, is merely a part of the fullness God holds out
to us in His Own life which He longs to live *in* us as we
go about in the daily patterns that make our lives *our*
lives. He longs to show Himself within the confines of
our personalities which form our friendships and set the
direction of our beliefs and influence our work on earth.
　God is willing to walk the earth again incarnate in
us.
　This thought is too high for me.
　I cannot attain to it.

But I can participate in it. Because of what the Lord Jesus has done on Calvary.

And as I dare to take part more and more in the very life of Christ which has been put within me, my heart leaps up in wonder each time I discover that contained in His life is so much more than the average Christian dreams of!

I confess to that stunted dream.

But I mean to break out of it more and more each day.

Books are written and sermons spoken on the pursuit of peace and constancy and faith and growth. Books should be written and sermons should be spoken on the tremendous fact that in Him all these things for which we all long *do* exist.

And yet, we should not stop with these.

The gift of the life of Jesus Christ within the believer is never quite discoverable in a long lifetime lived in looking *at* it from *outside*. Least of all by those of us who waited so long to receive it. My heart prompts me to waste no more time failing to look *inside* into unusual corners and under different lights in my search for more of the secret riches God offers us in the indwelling Christ!

". . . it pleased the Father that in him should all fulness dwell."

What more is there in this unspeakable fullness which is ours?

What treasures have we missed in the darkness of our own refusal to explore?

". . . I will give thee the treasures of darkness, and hidden riches of secret places. . . ."

How glad I am for His patience because darkness will come again and again into my life as it comes into every life, and even though I sulked at the darkness and forgot to look for the treasures during all those other times, He will be waiting to point them out when I look again at some other dark time still to come.

". . . I will give thee the treasures of darkness, and hidden riches of secret places. . . ."

Peace, faith, growth, constancy.

What of the other longings of my old life before Christ came in? What of the longings which had right origins, longings which even then came from God, but which He could not fulfill because I was cut off from Him by sin?

Your special longings may not be the same as mine. But I am inclined to think that mine will find a response in your heart and yours in mine. If they are longings that come from the heart of the God who created us both, this is bound to be true.

I would share with you four *particular* longings from my life before I turned to Christ *and* after. They did not change. They came from God.

And for brief, tempting periods in my life without Him, I touched these four things for which I longed. I cannot say I possessed them. I only touched them and found them good and then lost them again.

Each one.

Particularly did I long for these things as a writer. Writers have great need of all four of them. So do painters and composers and artists of any kind.

So do mothers and doctors.

And salesmen and teachers and missionaries.

Everyone may not be aware of the need, but everyone does have need of all four.

It so happened that I recognized my need of them. I also knew I lacked them most of the time, in spite of the fact that my longing kept right on.

I needed these things and longed for them before Christ came in.

I needed these things and longed for them after He came.

To my great surprise and delight and relief, I have now discovered that I have them!

They are mine every minute of every day and night and all I have to do to enjoy them is to partake as freely as I like!

They are all in Him.

They all came in abundance and to stay when He came in His fullness to stay forever.

And the first of these things for which I longed was *sensitivity*.

As a writer, I particularly needed to be sensitive to

the reactions and viewpoints and personalities of other people. Actually, as a writer of daytime serials, I obtained most of my contracts because I wrote what was called "sensitively realistic" dialogue. I have never said that I wrote dialogue as people really speak. I wrote as people *think* they speak! Or as they *think* others speak.

My child "characters" were supposed to be realistic.

They weren't. I knew practically nothing about children. I simply wrote what mothers *think* their children are like! Which, I suppose, is a kind of sensitivity to mothers. But, I will admit to a *limited amount* of true sensitivity in my *writing* during my old life, and there it stopped.

My "sensitivity" in the main, beyond radio dialogue, was in reality only *touchiness*!

Many confuse the two words.

Purposely.

Someone said to me not long ago: "Oh, I know God won't let me have to live with *her* again! He knows I'm far too sensitive to be around someone as crude as that."

Sensitive?

No.

Touchy.

When I first became a Christian, I simply could not attend a church where the soprano was likely to sing off key. I suffered too much at the hand of my "sensitive" nature if I did.

Sensitive?

No.

Touchy.

Do not misunderstand. The true sensitivity which came when Christ came in His fullness, the sensitivity which increases in me as I decrease, has made me a better radio director, a better writer, a better conversationalist. It has not made me deaf to the lady hiding behind the trembling anthem because her high c slipped. I can still hear her. I still know she didn't make it. But instead of squirming and feeling sorry for my own "sensitive" self, Someone *else* in me wants to *pray* for her and His influence makes *me* want to pray for her too!

Jesus Christ is all sensitivity.

No touchiness.

All sensitivity.

They are not the same.

If my feelings are easily hurt, that is no sign that I am sensitive in the true sense of the word.

But it is a sign that I'm touchy!

True sensitivity meets other people where *they* are. Jesus always met each person where the other person stood. He did not shade the truth in order to do it. He was the truth. He remained Himself, but He anticipated the other person's reactions to Him. He was sensitive to their heartaches, their twists, their sins. He put Himself in the position of having to say "thank you" to an immoral person when He asked the Samaritan woman at the well to give Him a drink of water. He asked her for a drink *first*. It did not excuse her sin. But it softened her heart toward Him a little and in return she gave Him her attention and He could give her living water.

He met her where she was, needing to think that someone needed her, even for a drink of water.

He was *sensitive* to her.

Because He is the origin of all sensitivity.

The Creator of every leaf sensitive to every wind.

". . . without him was not any thing made that was made."

The bird's quick eye and every gentle hand.

". . . by him all things consist."

Including the sensitivity for which I longed. And which I now have *only* because Christ lives in me. I knew it for brief, tempting times before He came. Enough to make me long for more. And more consistently.

Christians desperately need the very sensitivity of God. We need to see that although *we* have light, others may not. If we realize that we are all apt to stumble through a darkened room, even though it is a familiar room, we must be sensitive enough to see that those we may be trying to reach for Christ are still in darkness and the normal thing to do when it is dark is to stumble. And to look at things from a wrong perspective. People are off balance in a dark room. If we are sensitive with the sensitivity of Christ, we will not condemn or click our tongues at the man who drinks heavily. If he has not received Jesus Christ as His Saviour from sin, I wonder that he doesn't drink more! If we are sensitive with His sensitivity, we will not condemn the person whose starved emotions seek to be fed in an illicit relationship. We will remember that it is dark where that person is. Jesus Christ is the only light of the world.

Christians who expect those in whom Christ does *not* yet dwell to act as though He *does,* make His cross "much ado about nothing"! If we possess His sensitivity, we will not do this.

". . . where are those thine accusers? . . . Neither do I condemn thee: go, and sin no more."

My sensitivity need not come and go now that He has come to live in me.

It can remain constant.

Jesus Christ is the same today as He was yesterday and He will be just the same tomorrow.

And *He* is my sensitivity.

9. TO BE OBJECTIVE

When Christ came to live His life in me, He came a light into my self-dark world and in that light I have begun to see "hidden riches in the secret places" of our life together.

Riches for which I had longed. Sensitivity and now— *objectivity.*

Writers especially need to be objective.

As do mothers and doctors and teachers and missionaries.

As do people. If they are to live balanced, sane lives. Objectivity is very lacking in our world. Most of us are looking out *from* ourselves as we look out *for* ourselves. We are boxed off one by one by one in our extreme *subjectivity.*

"I'm this way because my grandfather was before me."

And his grandfather before him.

"I don't know . . . I haven't always been this way. It just seems like my life's so *hard!*"

And my mother before me.

"I'm *like* this . . . when the going gets too rough, I just have to get off by myself. I can't take confusion and other people's troubles! That's just the way I am."

And my father before me.

And the human race before *him*.

Looking out for *us* from the viewpoint of *ourselves*.

How I longed for *objectivity* in my life before Christ. How I longed in the very depths of my being to be objective about life. I remember very little else in James Joyce's book *The Portrait of the Artist As a Young Man,* but I do remember the gist of one very joycian declaration: *The true artist is one who sits in the corner and pares his fingernails as he works.*

I remember that declaration because it made me jealous for two reasons. First, I had no fingernails to pare! I had bitten my nails since childhood and no amount of parental cajoling and bribing had caused me to stop. (Fingernails came too when Christ came. And not until.) The second reason that declaration stirred me to jealousy was the thrilling picture of pure objectivity as the artist sat paring his fingernails in calm, unemotional appraisal of the very work he was creating!

An artist like that would be out of his own way.

What he had to say could come through. Of course, I had very little or nothing to say in those days, even if I could have captured and held that longed-for objectivity. I could be objective about words themselves, but when I began to put them together, my own garbled emotions got in the way. I was so subjective in my own personal life, I was all over the place when I wrote!

The only persons I knew who were *not* subjective and emotionally slopping over the sides of their efforts were those who had dropped love out of their vocabulary of living. Who had hardened into what they called "objectivity."

I wasn't quite that old yet.

I still wanted to be warm and loved and to love in return.

And so I circled around in my subjective circle, ringed around by myself. And longed for the freedom of being off my own hands and *objective*.

I knew my writing would be improved if I could stop taking personal pokes at the people I knew and begin setting down characterizations objectively from the corner as I "pared."

But I saw my "characters" from *my* viewpoint and I had so many grudges and criticisms and, of course, no nails to pare.

So, I kept on longing for the objectivity which I had now and then touched and then lost.

Objectivity and sensitivity, like peace, do not come in packages.

They come from within.

They are all contained *in* the One without whom nothing was made that was made.

Human beings can only be naturally objective toward things about which they do not care. I was nicely objective about Arabian oil, for example. And double-barreled shotguns.

My father and brother could get into heated, emotional upsets over shotguns, but guns left me cold. Therefore objective.

True objectivity is demonstrated only when we are able to remain undisturbed at the center of our beings in the midst of the crashing of our own defenses or the sound of our own breaking hearts. True art and true living come from such as this.

I was incapable of it.

Until He came. And with Him came my longed-for objectivity.

I no longer need to be ruled by my circumstances. I need no longer to be a victim of my emotions. Or the emotions of someone I love. Or dislike.

I am free at last to sit in the corner and pare the fingernails He gave me when He came, bringing my eternal life and my blessed objectivity for which I had longed.

Christ lives in me and I *can* be off my own hands and into His hands, looking and living and writing and loving from His point of view and no longer my own.

This is a great, great relief.

Jesus Christ . . . the only Person outside of ourselves who is attractive enough to pull us out of our subjective boxes and set us free to live—objectively!

". . . I will give thee the treasures . . . and hidden riches of secret places . . ." "I will not leave you comfortless: *I* will come to you."

And bring with Me *everything* you need.

"O God, thou art my God; early will I seek thee . . ."!

10. TO BE SIMPLIFIED

For as long as I can remember caring at all, I have been attracted by *simplicity*.

It has been well said that John, the Beloved Disciple, saw into the very heart of the gospel of Jesus Christ, when late in his earthly life, writing what we now know as his first letter, he framed the essence of the gospel in pure simplicity: ". . . *God is love.*"

I believe John had grown into that insight as the life of God increased in him and what he saw was *simplicity* itself!

How I longed for simplicity before I became a Christian. Little did I know I was longing for the very essence of the gospel of Christ! I would have laughed had anyone told me I longed for Christ Himself. I merely longed for simplicity knowing that all great art—painting, music, writing, sprang from simplicity itself. And so I longed for this simplicity in my own life so I could transfer it to my writing. Picasso's painting, Matisse's line drawings, Marin's water colors, Gertrude Stein's daring singleness of pen in which she allowed the *thing* to describe *itself,* made me strain with desire to capture the same brave simplicity for my own. You may laugh at Miss Stein's oft-quoted and oft-ridiculed line "a rose is a rose is a rose is a rose." But *is* a rose anything else but a rose? Doesn't a rose best describe itself?

I have known since I was old enough to care that the truly well-dressed woman is the *simply* dressed woman. A frantic scramble of flowers and veils and plastic bobs turns the eyes away for "rest" on something simpler! Our eyes are drawn *to* simplicity. This is natural because God made us to be at home in a world with large expanses of sky and ocean and mountains.

We *rest* in the wide-open spaces because they are *simpler* than the clutter and jerk of shapes and rattles in a city block.

The truly well-turned-out home is the simply decorated home. Too many ruffles in the kitchen curtains will claw at the splatter of wallpaper most likely designed by a neurotic craftsman who needs the *simplicity* of the gospel.

Of God Himself.

Do not misunderstand. Your taste in houses and dress have nothing to do with your growth in the Spirit of God! I use these merely to illustrate my own longing for simplicity.

Being aware that you may share it.

Of course, I could affect simplicity in my dress and houses before Christ came to live within me. But I threw away reams of paper seeking it in my writing.

Write, whittle, pare. Then throw it away.

Not simple enough.

Too many adjectives describing description itself! And failing often.

Now and then the thing I sought to say said itself as simply as I longed for it to do. But only now and then.

And almost never in my personal life was there simplicity at all.

Even then I knew I could never write simply and greatly until I had somehow become simplified. But I could only long for it. I was webbed around by the perpetual complication of a critical nature. By over-emotionalism. By unevenness of disposition. By a bumpy set of values based on too many things for simplicity. I struggled to master a simple writing style and then I had nothing simple and clear to say!

Everything seemed off-center and uneven and muddy.

And it seemed that way because it was.

As I was.

Now Christ lives in me. And with Him came the blessed simplicity for which I longed and struggled. I find I seldom think on simplicity now. I simply use it as I use my brain. It is a part of me. It came when He came. It is the needed single-eye *given* to those who would see Jesus Christ as He is. The Holy Spirit knows about this needed single-eye and, of course, He gives it to us when He knows we are willing to accept it!

To use it.

To dare to see what is possible even for *us* on this earth with Christ living in us. To dare to look at who it is living there!

A great, restful, simplification sweeps into the life that is truly given over in every area to Jesus Christ. We stop going seven directions at once. We are pulled together into one whole.

Excesses are lopped off.

The way *is* blessedly narrow, we discover with a shout of joy!

No need to lose our way now because there is only one road like this one and it is single and simple and straight and leads to eternal fulfillment for the most limited among us.

Eternal fulfillment of everything for which you long.

Of everything for which I long.

Simplicity.

"Come unto *me*. . . ."

". . . *I* am the way. . . ."

". . . Follow *me*. . . ."

". . . *I* will come to you."

". . . *I* will dwell in them, and walk in them. . . ."

". . . *I* will come in. . . ."
Simplicity.
No confusion. Only one way to go. Where He goes.
Jesus Christ Himself is my simplicity.

11. TO BE ORIGINAL

To me, this is the perfect sentence in all recorded literature:

"In the beginning was the Word, and the Word was with God, and the Word was God."

Its content is the greatest.

Its style is the greatest.

Its impact upon history and upon me greater than any other because it seems to contain all that God is.

All of God that *can* be contained in words.

These words go beyond themselves. They are simpler than simplicity. Deeper than deep. Higher than height itself.

They are *purely original.*

They contain God and they come from God.

God Himself, through the Holy Spirit, directed John, the Beloved Disciple, to write them. As he wrote them.

Only God could have directed a sentence like that.

Only God knew how things were "in the beginning."

"In the beginning God created the heaven and the earth . . . ," *but* only God could have known that *with* Him, as He Created, was the Word, Jesus Christ. That ". . . the Word *was* God."

"And the Word was made flesh, and dwelt among us. . . ."

Only God knew the content of John's second sentence in his Gospel: "The same was in the beginning *with God*." Only God could have written the third sentence: "All things were made by him; and without him was not any thing made that was made."

The writing itself in those three verses would make a human writer give up if that writer did not believe God wrote them! They contain perfect writing. Impossible to man. And perfect truth.

And they contain the sublime proof that still another of my old longings has been met in the Person of Jesus Christ dwelling within me. *Originality.*

Even before I could recognize it as such, when I was a very small child, I must have been longing to be original. As I grew older, this turned to disaster. My "originality" became troublesome "individuality" with its elbows out in every direction!

At nineteen I was too old in boredom for my years. And eccentric.

At twenty I had almost run out of ways to be "different."

And yet, I truly believe that longing came *originally*

from God. Everyone longs to be original. If we make a little hopeful joke, we enjoy the warm wave that rises when someone is kind enough to laugh. If we write a little poem—even one we know should not be graced with the name of poetry—we want it to be admired and thought fresh and different. Women like to be thought original in planning parties and wardrobes and dinners and husbands. Men like to be thought original when they tell you "by the yard" after dinner just what happened on that trip last summer, often explaining longer than the color movies of it which they also hope are original. Children love to plan surprises. Any kind. From Easter baskets to lovely dead frogs under your covers at night.

The longing for originality is good.

It comes from God.

What we do with it can come straight from His enemy!

I longed for originality as a writer. This was good. It made me diligent when I might have been just vain and careless. And some of the time there *was* originality in what I wrote. And in the way it was written. But only some of the time.

As with sensitivity and objectivity and simplicity I was only able to catch at it and watch it go. I longed to be original. Consistently original.

New.

102

Spring was a fact. It always came. And it was always new. But I wasn't. I was getting old. In everything.

And then Christ came to live within me.

The same Jesus Christ who *was* in the beginning . . . who was with God and who *was* God! In me, in me, in me, *this* Christ?

Yes.

". . . I will come in. . . ."

The One without whom nothing was made that was made!

The great Creator God had come to live in *me*.

Had become my Saviour and my Holy Guest forever.

Jesus Christ was not another *creation of God*. He was there when all creation was created! He is the One who made all the heavens and all the worlds and all the universes and all that each contains.

He, who created *me lives* in me.

This is too high for me. I cannot attain unto it. But I can accept it and begin to partake of the originality that springs from Origin itself!

I need never run short of ideas.

I need never *force* another idea as long as I live.

I need only to take of the very life of the Creator God. And that life is in me.

Christ Himself in me . . . my *only* hope of originality.

Never a copy.

103

Never a duplication.

One constant new beginning with the One who was there "before the world was." Who said: ". . . before the day was I am He. . . ."

I no longer need to struggle to be original.

". . . without him was not any thing made that was made. . . ."

And He lives in me.

Forever.

12. I LONGED TO KNOW HIM
AS HE IS!

I shall know Him, I shall know Him,
As redeemed by His Side I shall stand . . .
I shall know Him, I shall know Him,
By the print of the nails in His Hand!

If you have ever sung this old gospel song, you know what I mean when I say that when I reach the line: "As redeemed by His Side I shall stand" . . . I am not at all surprised at the next line which repeats the irrevocable fact that we *will* know Him when we stand one day by His side—redeemed! But those of us who have been redeemed by the love and the blood that flowed from the cross of Calvary know that if we had not been *redeemed* we most certainly would *not* know Jesus Christ!

We simply do not *recognize* something with which we have no ties and no affinity.

No resemblance.

Those of us who have come to know Jesus Christ as our own *personal* redeemer, know that we, in our unredeemed selves can have *no* family likeness to our Saviour! But we also know that when He comes to dwell within us . . . when we receive Him as our Saviour and then permit Him to take us over and master us, there begins to be an actual family resemblance. That this could be in *us* as we are and Jesus Christ as He *is*, is the wonder of redemption. And yet, does He not come actually to live His life in our bodies when we receive Him?

Either He does or Jesus Himself was not sure of His ground when He said that *if* we would open the door He would come in. That He would send the comforter. That He Himself would come.

Those of us who are "learning of" Jesus Christ know that He was and is very sure of His ground. If we have received Him with sincere hearts, He *has come in*!

We *can* begin to resemble Him.

Not because we are learning how to be Christ-like, but because we are gradually permitting Him to rule our lives! He never lives contradictory to Himself. The Spirit of Jesus Christ is always unmistakably the Spirit of Jesus Christ.

The Spirit of Jesus Christ is always unmistakably the Spirit of Jesus Christ!

Christian work does not make us resemble Christ.

Christian church attendance does not make us resemble Christ.

Christian thoughts do not make us resemble Christ.

Christian witnessing does not make us resemble Christ.

The actual indwelling presence of Jesus Christ makes us resemble Him and nothing else can counterfeit this likeness!

"Take my yoke upon you and learn of me. . . ."

I say I long to know Him as He is.

You may say, "What if I don't *want* to learn of Jesus Christ? What if there is no desire within me to 'learn of Him.' What then?"

If He is within you, ask Him to *create* the desire *for* you. After all, if He created you, can He not create a *desire* within you? If Jesus Christ tells us (and He does) to "learn of Him," would He be the kind of God we know Him to be when we look at Him on the cross, if He did not intend to change us until our very desires were His desires for us?

He can convert our desires too.

He can actually *become* our desire!

Do you think for one minute that Paul had a corner on the market of the burning heart? To Paul as Saul of Tarsus, "to live" was *not* Jesus Christ until this same Jesus Christ made it so! He creates in us the desire to know Him and then fulfills that desire for us. Saul of

107

Tarsus might have shouted "To me to live is to *persecute* this Jesus Christ!"

When Saul, the destroyer, was transformed into Paul, the disciple, he cried out of a heart that had been healed and filled with a hunger for still further healing: "That *I may know him* . . ."!

"That I may know him, and the power of his resurrection, and the fellowship of his sufferings, being made comformable unto his death"!

We know, even as we sing through the wobbly verse of the dear old song about knowing Him "as redeemed by His Side we shall stand," that *then* in that day when we do see Him face to face, *we shall know Him* . . . but what of now?

Can we know Jesus Christ now?

Really know Him?

Yes.

We *can* know Him now.

The spirit within us witnesses to His Spirit within us that we are children of God.

Citizens of heaven.

Still living on this old earth at our address!

You, living where you live, and being named your name, *can* know Jesus Christ. Otherwise He would not have said, ". . . learn of me. . . ." He does not urge us to the impossible with Himself. He urges us to follow Him and then proves to us that nothing is impossible with God.

108

I long to know Him as He is.

To know Him is to live.

"In him was life. . . ."

". . . I am the bread of life. . . ."

". . . the water that I shall give him shall be in him a well of water springing up into everlasting life . . ."

"If any man thirst, let him come unto me, and drink."

To know Him is to know life. "And this is life eternal, that they might know . . . Jesus Christ whom thou hast sent."

To know Him!

As He is.

"As the hart panteth after the water brooks, so panteth my soul after thee, O God."

Living with Him and knowing that He lives in me have made me long to know Him better. As He is!

With Augustine I cry . . . "My heart is restless until it rests in thee!"

Seeking to know Him as He is.

Not as He has been described, but as He is.

Longing to know Him beyond the printed page. Beyond the spoken word.

Beyond.

He Himself planted that longing within me. In His kindness which is always all around me, He shows me *how* I may know Him . . . as He is.

He shows me carefully and clearly, as He had showed Paul when he wrote: "That I may know him, and the power of his resurrection, and the fellowship of his sufferings, being made conformable unto his death."

In this cry from the heart of Paul, the bondslave of Jesus Christ, we find clearly set forth the *only* way to *know* Him. As He is.

For the next three chapters we will attempt to show that knowing Jesus Christ as He is, personally, is only *three steps away* from us all.

It is my prayer that you will be given the power to *take* these three steps into the life He wants you to live!

13. ENOUGH TO BE MADE NEW?

"That I may know him . . ."!

The cry from the heart of St. Paul is still rising from the hearts of those of us who long to know Jesus Christ as He is. In Philippians 3:10, Paul exclaims: "That I may know him, and the power of his resurrection, and the fellowship of his sufferings, being made conformable unto his death."

If we do *not* long to know Him, this verse is an anathema. It sticks in our spiritual throats and we cough and sputter and try to forget at least the last two steps set forth so clearly in the verse that vibrates with Paul's own personal longing after the One who had transformed his life. But the cry within this one verse contains the three steps into *Oneness* with Jesus Christ.

The three steps into peace.

Into victorious living.

Into the joy He promised the night they were planning to kill Him.

111

Into some knowledge of what He is really like.

Three distinct steps away and yet no one step can be taken without the other two! One step must follow and one step must precede and there is no real beginning and no real ending. In this sense they are not steps at all, they are parts of a circle which completes itself as Christ completes the human heart.

If within our hearts He has been allowed to plant the longing for Himself, we leap to embrace this verse, rejoicing even in the thorns in it which pierce and tear as the hard, young buds break open in our souls and the perfume of maturing flowers causes us to forget the blood upon the thorns was ever ours.

The blood was never ours,
'Twas ever His!

And because He walked *out* of that blood-soaked, borrowed tomb that first Easter morning, He is alive today to walk *into* the tomb of our lives. And as He comes *within* such light breaks *upon* us and *within* us that we drop "darkness" from the words we know and vow never to use it again!

When *He* comes within! When we begin really to *believe* in the resurrection, because we have come to *know* Him who arose bodily and who now lives at the right hand of the Father *and* in us . . . praying, praying, pressing, pressing, pressing ever nearer, His Spirit working within the once-dark depths of our beings to make clean and bright the place where He will dwell.

The resurrection?

Yes. But still more—the One who arose!

"That I may know him, and the power of his resurrection. . . ."

This is the *first step* into Oneness with Jesus Christ.

That I may *know* Him in the power of His resurrection!

I do not shudder at this step. It grips me. It thrills me.

No one will shrink from the possession of power. We live in a power-crazed world. In fact, the phrase "power-crazed" is so trite we pass it over with no reaction at all. Political power. Economic power. Military power. Automotive power. Atomic power. Hydrogen power. The "power" of thinking in this direction and that. The "power of the press."

Just words. Almost.

But not unattractive words. We'll *take* power, most of us. Especially Americans love power. And most especially they love it if it is under the hood of their automobiles as they madly try to crowd each other into eternity on their super highways designed to help along the process. Oh, we'll take the first step gladly. We'll open wide our arms and our souls and *take* the ". . . power of his resurrection . . ."!

Is this true?

Will we do that?

Do we really long to know Him as He is?

Are we truly willing to be *given* a new life in Jesus Christ? Especially when it means we have to give up our old ones in exchange? Are we willing to be made new?

Are we really willing to be made new?

Are we willing to be given a brand-new life and not just use our own will power to "turn over a new leaf"? Resurrection power is the same power that brought the dead body of Jesus up out of that tomb! Do we want that to happen to us?

Right in the midst of things?

The power that invades us from above when we receive the life of God into our lives is the very same power that brought Jesus to life again. When we are born again from above, we are given life from the dead.

When we become Christians by the invasion of the Holy Spirit, we are brought to life! Eternal life.

And it is surely life out of death!

Because it is resurrection life and resurrection means life from death.

But sometimes it is comfortable to be dead.

To be alive means we have to move.

To know Him is to know life. We have said this. We say it again . . . *to know Jesus Christ is to know life itself!*

"And this is life eternal, that they might know thee the only true God, and Jesus Christ whom thou hast sent."

To be raised from the dead means "sleepers awake!"
To be raised from the dead means to be made new.
Why does it?

Because the Lord Jesus said, ". . . I am the resurrection, and the life . . ." and then He added, ". . . Behold, I make *all things new* . . ."!

Are we willing to be brought to life?

The next two steps tell the tale. The seed of His life must be planted in us by the Holy Spirit upon our turning to Christ, and this is the seed of resurrection life because He *is* the resurrection and the life. And so step one . . . "That I may know him, and the power of his resurrection . . ." must go before steps two and three: ". . . and the fellowship of his sufferings, being made conformable unto his death."

But . . . as a circle completes itself, so must steps two and three go before as well as follow step one!

The seed of the resurrection life must be *put within* us at conversion, but in order that we may go on to ". . . know him, and the POWER of his resurrection . . ." (that is, the *full* power . . . enough for victorious living "in the midst of") we must needs take steps two and three!

We need His life within us to be *enabled* to embrace the fellowship of His sufferings. And surely we need His life within us even to be *willing* to be ". . . made conformable unto his death"!

And so, all follow and yet all come before.

115

All are one and yet there are three.

"That I may know him . . . (1) and the power of his resurrection, (2) and the fellowship of his sufferings (3) being made conformable unto his death."

Do I long to know Him enough to take the first step? To be made new? To be willing to give up those old thought habits and personality tricks which Jesus Christ would not use?

Am I willing to stop using the "methods" I've used so long to "get my own way"?

Am I willing to stop hitting the pagans I know over the head with my doctrine in order to win them to *my point of view*? Will I begin to win them to Christ by letting Him make *me* new in my disposition so that He can love them *through* me?

Am I willing to change jobs if this one is against God? Or am I willing to stay with this one, knowing the ground on which I stand *is* Holy ground? In spite of my boss's disposition and the fact that I end up doing other people's work!

Am I willing to be made new?

To tell my "beloved story" for the very last time?

Never to indulge in that secret sin once more throughout all eternity?

Am I willing to give up the luxury of worry and the self-indulgence of fear?

Am I willing to be made *entirely new*?

Even to writing that letter or preparing dinner for

116

that person who, of all God's creatures, is the most difficult for me to "take"?

"... *Behold, I make all things new.* ..."

Do we still long to know Him if He says that to us *once more*?

"Remember ye not the former things, neither consider the things of old. Behold, I will do a new thing. ..."

"... Behold I make all things new."

Do we want to know Him enough for that?

14. ENOUGH TO SUFFER?

We have been facing the three steps set down *too clearly* by St. Paul in the tenth verse of the third chapter of his letter to the Philippians.

I say "too clearly" because there can be no begging the question, nor dodging the central issue in the way Paul set them down. And so, for those of us who *want* to beg a question or dodge an issue or hold onto a handful of rights to ourselves, it would be a convenience if the great Apostle had not made it so simple.

We could ponder it all.

We could claim confusion.

We could argue another interpretation.

And still another.

We could stall for time by pleading lack of understanding.

The Holy Spirit directed Paul to make it simple, though.

And He did.

God wants to be One with us. He wants us to long to know Him as He is. He knows we cannot know Him until we are near Him. And so He directed Paul to make it very clear to us. Paul did this in Philippians 3:10. Here we do not find three *easy* steps. But we do find three *clear* steps.

Three clear steps into Oneness with Jesus Christ.

Into knowing Him as He is.

Too clear, if we are fighting His claim to supremacy in our lives.

Blessedly clear to those of us who have been brought to the place of seeing once and for all that without Him we *can* do nothing!

Blessedly clear to those of us whose hearts ache to know more of this Jesus Christ who, by His Holy Spirit has *put* not only a "new song" into our hearts, but has made it a love song that sobs at times because we long more deeply for our beloved.

And then the longing deepens as He works within us.

And deepens.

And when it is deep *enough*, from "step one," when our hearts cried, "That I may know him, and the power of his resurrection . . ."! He leads us right up to "step two," "That I may know him, . . . and the fellowship of his sufferings. . . ."

We can't always *see* the path along which we are walking toward this step. More often than not our eyes are too filled with tears and everything all around us is

119

blurred and distorted because no one can focus clearly through tears. But He can see. And He leads us right up to "step two":

Entering into ". . . the fellowship of his sufferings. . . ."

He stands there beside us and our soul seems to hear Him say: "I know this is one of the steps you wish I hadn't made quite so clear through Paul when he wrote that letter to My children in Philippi. I understand why you're weeping. I understand why you're trying to miss this step. Near the top of Calvary there was a sunken place in the ground where another cross had stood. When they filled it in, some of the earth piled up to the right of it. I could have stumbled over that little rise in the ground. My eyes were filled with tears as yours are now. If I had stumbled it might have postponed the cross a minute longer. But I didn't *need* to stumble. I had prayed that *prayer* back there in the garden. It was all in the Father's hands. And He was with me. He was *in* me. I *could* have stumbled. I could have called for angel help. But I didn't *need* to and so I just went on and *took* that next step. And then I was at the top of the hill where the crucifixion was to take place. Believe me, My child, I do understand the way you feel about this step right here."

". . . the fellowship of his sufferings. . . ."

An attractive woman named Fannie Davis lived and loved through eleven near-perfect years with her husband, Bill, who was a peace officer in Abilene, Kansas. They both belonged to Jesus Christ, who seemed literally to hold them together in their marriage which anyone knew *had* truly been made in heaven. Made by the One who fed their love for Himself and for each other as they walked heart to heart with each other and heart to heart with Him through those wonderful eleven years. And then in 1949 the rest of us read in our newspapers of the peace officer named Bill Davis, who had been shot to death by an insane man barricaded in a burning house, near Abilene.

The police had to sift the ashes after the fire was put out in order to find Bill's badge for identification.

Fannie Davis stood at that "second step" trying to see *something* in it all that made sense!

She understood why tears were called "scalding tears" when people wrote stories about great weeping. She understood about those who spoke of trying to *"see through tears."*

She couldn't "see" at all.

Everywhere she looked there was a black agony that refused even to express *itself* and nothing penetrated it.

But He had led her there. He had not caused her husband's tragic death any more than His Father had caused *His* tragic death on Calvary. But He was *with* Fannie at that "second step" very near the top of the little hill, where her cross stood. And as He promised, He didn't leave her for a minute.

121

". . . lo, I am with you alway. . . ."

Fannie Davis was faced with the decision to *accept* Bill's death. To accept it and not *fight* it. And then to *take* that "second step" into the fellowship of the sufferings of her Lord willingly, in *His strength*! She still couldn't see a thing. But He could. And she *knew* He was there. Even when she didn't feel His presence. He had said He would never leave her nor forsake her. He was God. He didn't misrepresent things. He was there to give her His hand and to pour into her weak, weary, grief-blinded heart and mind and body, His very Own life . . . His power . . . the same power that enabled Him to take that last step at the top of another Calvary so long ago. The same power that ended that prayer in the Garden, and made all prayer forever afterward so simple that even a child can pray.

Fannie Davis took the "second step."

By His grace, which overflowed each minute, she *took* the "second step" in blind faith. But she took it. That's the important thing.

She *took* the step into the "fellowship of his sufferings" and once she had taken it, *her* "radiant moment" broke from eternity into her time-shackled life.

"I was able to sit through my beloved Bill's funeral service *knowing* a feeling of genuine exhilaration! I knew Bill was *not* dead. I knew as I had never known before that Jesus Christ was not dead. That He and Bill were together forever. And forever alive!"

Fannie Davis took the "second step" and she *knew* *Him* in a new way from that moment on!

In the next chapter, we will look at how this same woman took the third step into Oneness with Jesus Christ ". . . being made conformable unto his death."

We shudder at entering into the fellowship of His sufferings.

We *balk* outright at being made conformable to His death.

But the steps are clear. The call is clear. God knows about these things that we face. And once we have taken all three steps . . . *we* no longer demand to know!

Our questions turn to praise because at last we *know* Him!

"That I may know him, and the power of his resurrection, and the fellowship of his sufferings, being made conformable unto his death."

Do I long to know Him enough to suffer and *accept* the suffering?

15. ENOUGH TO DIE?

"I have tried and tried and tried to make Jesus Christ become real to me! After reading your autobiography *The Burden Is Light,* I am filled with a deeper longing to know Him as He really is. But the more I try, the farther away He seems to be! I force myself to pray for longer periods of time. I keep more frequent devotional times. I pray up and down my prayer list. I give more to God's work than a tithe. I attend all church services and activities possible. I have pictures of Christ in every room in my house. I try to keep my promises to Him . . . Oh, Genie Price, I just try and try and try to get Him to be real to me and I fail miserably! Why should life be like this? What am I to do?"

You are to die.

Did I send this terse reply to the sincere letter which I have just quoted? No, not in those brief four words. I have learned that the quick, glib answer only deepens

124

wounds kept open by self-deception or self-pity or lack of light. This kind of wound is one of the most painful of all.

And it is also one of the most common of all.

It is a wound made usually from years of *unconscious* living for oneself and it is usually infected by the germ of *unconscious* self-pity. But its most striking characteristic is that it *cannot* heal.

This kind of wound in the human personality cannot heal over because it is not *exposed* to the light.

This person writes in darkness.

Not from conscious sin. More from ignorance.

All this wild, flailing, frantic effort to *try* to make Christ real only increases the irritation.

But by some means coerce or drag or draw this sincerely seeking, but completely self-deceived person out into the light that streams from the cross of Calvary and if he or she will expose the wound long enough—it will begin to heal!

The suffering, seeking saint will see that *death* is the answer.

Death and *healing* together?

Can these two meet on any ground?

They *have* met on the blood-soaked ground beneath the cross on which Jesus Christ died. And they met again in the flower-filled garden in which the birds sang around an empty tomb no one expected even to be opened again.

The rough, splintery cross on which they nailed Him was real.

The blood He shed as He poured out His very life for our sakes was real.

The nails were real.

The thorns were real.

The spear was real. And the vinegar.

The bawdy jokes were real and the suffocation in His heart as He smothered our sin. *The sin was real!*

But the One who *took* the sin into His Own heart was real also.

And He still is.

Because the tomb is open?

No. The tomb is open and empty because He was and *is* real!

The tomb is open because He is the one *true* God.

True and real.

And alive. Could God stay dead?

Jesus Christ is alive and sitting at the right hand of the Father, praying for you and for me and for the pathetic person who so completely had missed the point as he wrote that letter in the dark!

Jesus Christ is alive and very, very real to those who know Him. *He is real even if no one knew Him.* But to those of us who are beginning to know Him as He is, He becomes more real as we embrace the truth that the life He offers *is* life out of death.

Eternal life is *life* from *death*.

Resurrection life is *life* from *death.*

We must be made conformable to his death!

What does that mean?

It means many things, but for our practical discussion now, it means that you and I must be willing to die out to every personality trait or trick . . . to every mode of thought . . . to every way of life . . . to every relationship . . . to every ambition . . . to *everything* that is not found in the personality and character of Jesus Christ!

We can try until we are spiritually "blue in the face," as the writer of the letter has done, to *make* Jesus Christ real. We can try and try and try to know Him in the power of His resurrection . . . we can suffer agonies as we picture Him suffering on the cross of Calvary . . . we can go with Him bravely through personal tragedy, enduring with clenched teeth so no one will find out that *our* Christianity is not working! We can "protect" Jesus Christ's reputation before others by feigning a chin-up deliverance from grief . . . we can do all of these things until we *are* "blue in the face." And we will only end up with "spiritual blues" unless we die to our SELVES!

Unless we do this, we are merely protecting our *selves!*

". . . Except a corn of wheat fall into the ground and die, it abideth alone: but if it *die,* it bringeth forth much fruit."

Jesus said that Himself. And as always He said in a few words what we complicate by many words.

No living, growing wheat waves in any Kansas wheat field *until* the corn of wheat has first *died*.

Even Jesus Christ could not be glorified until after He died, so why should we pine away good hours *trying* to "get Him" to be glorified in us, until *we* die too?

Jesus also said, ". . . I, if I be lifted up from the earth (on the cross), will *draw* all men unto me." The unredeemed human "self" swaggering about laughing at the idea of itself on a cross, is a repulsive "self." Even other unredeemed "selves" find it unattractive because they want to do the swaggering! The unsurrendered "Christian self" is oftentimes *more* repulsive! But the sinful, selfish, swaggering human SELF "lifted up on a cross" with Christ—*draws!* This sweetened self is free to *walk* quietly and surely through tragedy and grief and hardship and heartache. It does not have to waste energy by swaggering. It is crucified with Christ . . . but it *is* strangely *alive*. Marvelously alive because Christ Himself lives in that redeemed, radiant self.

With many of us this death to self can be effected on the surrender of *one central issue*. It may be that in your life there is one person, one ambition, one habit, one desire, one right to yourself to which you cling doggedly. And as long as you cling to that one "thing" or person you cannot live freely as crucified with Christ. You give

128

most of your old self to be made conformable to His death, but not quite all. You are *almost* on the cross. But one hand waves free, clutching whatever symbol you hold dearer than knowing Jesus Christ!

In our last chapter, we told the story of Fannie Davis, who entered gloriously and realistically into the fellowship of the suffering of Jesus Christ, when she *accepted* the death of her beloved husband, Bill, in the spirit of Christ. Fannie Davis amazed her friends. They expected her to collapse. But in her acceptance she had come to know her Lord more deeply and *He held her.*

But without meaning to be stubborn, she told me she *had* insisted that God permit her at least to continue living in the house she and Bill had built and decorated together. She stayed on there for six years. But her life was not unfolding. She longed to know Jesus Christ better. She prayed earnestly that He would lead her into some new work that would help fill her maimed life. No answer seemed to come. There was only silence.

Until Fannie Davis let go of her insistence that God "at least" allow her to live on in the house she loved so much! That house was the symbol of Fannie's right to herself. And when she gave it back to God, she died out completely to her old self! Almost at once a fine position opened in which this authentic Christian life can touch the lives of thousands of teen-agers! When Fannie *died,* she *rose!*

Now, she has to leave her beloved house and move to a strange city where she knows few people. But she is walking with Jesus without strain.

She *knows* Him.

She has died with Him and now, in the fullness of life with Him, she will draw to herself, with simple, unconscious grace, a new circle of friends . . . an entirely new and fruitful life.

". . . Except a corn of wheat . . . die, it abideth alone. . . ."

Do you really want to know Jesus Christ as He is?

If you do . . . if I do . . . we will, by His grace, step into the power of His resurrection then enter into the fellowship of His sufferings . . . and not protest when He calls us even to the death of the cross.

He has been there first.

And where He is . . . and *only* where He is, will we find the true desires of our hearts met at last.

"That I may know him, and the power of his resurrection, and the fellowship of his sufferings, being made conformable unto his death."

Do I long to know Him enough to die?

16. STOP LONGING AND DIE!

Do I long to know Him enough to die?

If you honestly believe that you do, and yet you seem unable to die or to stay dead, read on. Right now, you no doubt think my chapter title is glib and unfeeling and smug. Perhaps you are wondering about me. What right have I to tell you to stop longing and die?

Have I done it?

No!

I tried for five years of my Christian life and ended up exactly where you may be right now—living in a state of constantly attempted suicide! I have "reckoned myself to be dead unto sin and alive unto God" until I was nothing but exhausted and that is just what the enemy hoped I would be. You too.

But doesn't the Bible tell us to ". . . reckon (ourselves) to be dead indeed unto sin, but alive unto God . . ."?

Yes.

Then what's wrong?

131

I am witnessing again. So many deep and wise and light-filled essays and books and commentaries have been written on this very subject that I almost hesitate to touch on it myself. I am not learned and I am not an authority on anything except what I have tried in my own life and found to be true.

And workable.

And free for the asking. For anyone.

My only value to you is this: If a thing works for me, it can also work for you. No one, absolutely no one has a corner on the market of the freedom that always follows "... the law of the Spirit of life in Christ Jesus. ..."

No one with a string of theological degrees after his name has an "exclusive."

And certainly not I.

But let me try to tell you step by step how I came to the beginning of a new freedom. I say to the *beginning* of a new freedom, because it is still opening before me every day.

I see no end to it.

Because there is none. It is eternal and that is forever.

For the first five years of my own Christian life, and particularly for three of them, I "reckoned."

Sometimes I reckoned calmly. Or tried to.

Sometimes I reckoned with great vigor.

Sometimes I reckoned with high feeling.

Sometimes I reckoned with no feeling at all.

At other times I just—reckoned.

But within a day or two, or occasionally within an hour or two after the great "reckoning" had taken place, I would find myself quite alive to—pitying myself for my heavy schedule or forcing my opinion on someone while cutting him down to size spiritually.

In other words, I found myself still quite alive to sin.

What was wrong? I believe I was trying to bring a certain state of my inner-life into being by *means of my reckoning.*

In other words I was still attempting suicide.

And not making it.

Looking back now, I see there were two reasons why I was not making it. First of all, I am always going to have a *self.* The point is not to kill myself, but to die to the down-pull of indulging that self according to her earth-bound instincts! The other reason why I believe I failed was that I was reckoning on my *reckoning.*

I was reckoning on my reckoning.

Now, this is not new at all. You may have read it in a dozen other books. After all, it is in the Bible. We are not to reckon ourselves to be dead . . . but dead to the *need* to give in to temptation.

In other words, we *can* pass a "point of no return." Trans-oceanic airplanes carry enough fuel to bring them back to their take-off point should they develop engine trouble *up* to a certain distance. Beyond that point, if the trouble develops, they have to hit for their destination. They have passed "the point of no return." I came to see gradually and joyfully and somewhat nervously that this was also true for Christians! We too could pass a "point of no return." I was nervous because I was quite attached to some of the things which I saw I could be finished with forever.

For only one small example, I found quite a bit of delight still in explaining to God in my prayers how far short of the Christian ideal certain of my co-workers fell. This made me feel "spiritual" by comparison. I liked the feeling. As I still liked the relief of alibis and excuses when I failed to do something I should have done.

The idea of never permitting myself the luxury of "humbly worded" destructive criticism again nor the release of "putting someone in her place" made me quite nervous.

I trembled inwardly as I had trembled outwardly the day I faced the fact that I *could,* because of God's provision for me on Calvary, go through all eternity without ever smoking even one more cigarette. Cigarettes meant that much to me.

That moment still shakes me and five years of that eternity without a cigarette have passed.

I want you to see that I understand your trembling at the prospect that it is quite possible for you never to give in to that particular temptation again as long as you live. And that is forever.

My "reckoning," however sincere, had not worked for at least two reasons. I was trying to kill off an eternal self and I was reckoning on my "reckoning." My self is eternal. It is to be "alive unto God" and only "dead unto sin." Reckoning on my own "reckoning" is a squirrel-cage procedure. I walk to the wall and snap on the light in my workroom "reckoning" on the *fact* that the switch is connected and the current is there waiting. I do not reckon on my reckoning about the current. I reckon on the *current*.

The day God showed me that was a big day.

Did I not believe that Jesus Christ had done a finished work on Calvary? That the power to forgive and break the power of sin in my life was let loose that day? Wasn't the current there waiting?

Yes. I wept for joy. And trembled some more.

And then, with this new light streaming, I began to re-read Galatians in my morning quiet time. I read through the first chapter. Then I began the second.

Soon I was reading one of the *first verses* I had memorized when I was trying to bring my lazy memory back to life right after I was converted.

I meant to read the whole verse.

Something stopped me.

Over and over the first two and a half lines my eyes ran.

"I am crucified with Christ: nevertheless I live; yet not I, but Christ liveth in me. . . ."

Over and over and over.

Then I could not get past the first phrase.

"I am crucified with Christ. . . ."

"I am crucified with Christ. . . ."

My heart leapt up!

I am *already* crucified with Christ!

This thing has been *done*. The part of me that *can* respond to sin has already been killed off. They not only killed Jesus on the cross, I was there too. He took me with Him!

I can't crucify myself. I'm too chickenhearted and selfish!

How many times had I said from how many platforms that no one can imitate Jesus Christ? And yet I had been trying in one sense to do what only He could have done.

This began to link up in my mind with other fragments of this great truth which He had been trying to teach me and I saw that if I am *willing* to know Him in the power of His resurrection, I *can*! I *can* be made conformable to His death because He has already taken not only my sin but my sinful, hard-to-handle ego to the cross with Him. Being made conformable merely means I take by faith what has already been done for me!

Suddenly being made conformable to His death lost its sting!

All my question marks about "reckoning" myself to

136

be dead were "straightened out and turned into exclamation points!"

Paul was not trying to make me miserable by holding up a standard for me to *reach*! He was witnessing to his own experience. He was handing me a standard in Galatians 2:20 which I could simply *take* for myself!

Would I dare?

Could it be this simple?

Was there no more need to struggle? I had read that. And at that moment I was able to confess for the first time that every time I read it, I grew rebellious and angry because *I* was still struggling. People told me their struggles were much more intense than mine. Some of them seemed almost to resent me because my Christian life was working at all. But I knew I had been struggling for a perpetually, minute-by-minute victorious life and at this point when the new light came, I trembled and wondered if I dare begin to act as though Galatians 2:20 were for me too!

I confess now that any time I had noticed another Christian writing Galatians 2:20 after his name in a book or at the close of a letter, I thought—"How does he *dare* do that?"

I was afraid to write it after an autograph in one of my books. For fear someone would say, "Crucified with Christ? She doesn't act like it!" Suddenly I was free to do it. Because I saw at last that it had to do with me too. I was no longer "reckoning" so that something new *would* happen. I was reckoning on something that had already happened!

On the fact of Calvary.

Psychologists and theologians use many and varied terms to express the essential *self*. I am not entering the field of controversy here at all. I do not wish to get into a discussion as to whether we have one, two, or twenty-two natures. I only know that my essential *self* needed to be redeemed. Needed to be made new. Needed desperately to have all the "old things pass away."

And I also know that the part of me which responds to sin was handled once and for all on Calvary—*if* I take hold of that fact by faith and use it!

I also know that my new self needs to be daily and hourly *aware* that *it is in the living presence of the Christ who dwells in me.*

More of that in the next two chapters. Here, I would have you see that the first instruction in Romans 6:11 is merely for us to *declare* by our actions that we have already been crucified with Christ. We reckon ourselves to be dead indeed unto sin because we *are*. And to bring this into reality so we can notice it in our daily lives, we need only to take it by faith and begin to *act* on it.

Here is a simple example of how that works.

Not long after I began to see and realize by faith this great freedom from "perpetually attempted suicide," I spoke at length on it at one of my favorite Bible conferences at Cannon Beach, Oregon. I had told my friends there of having read about a missionary who received a card from a friend on which was written this message: "Happy Birthday, I hope you *know* you're dead!"

We were emphasizing the need to *know* of our co-crucifixion with Christ.

Cannon Beach Conference out on the Pacific Ocean is different from most, because there I have a chance to let the people who come share with me what God is teaching them. We all grow from it. And one morning an extremely attractive lady shared this experience with us.

The night before, she had invited several people from the Conference for a supper after the evening service. The woman confessed to having always been extremely particular. Even when entertaining guests for a bedtime snack, she remained, in her own words "a fussy hostess." She wanted everything to be "just right." She confessed also that although she had been a Christian for a long time, she occasionally gave a waiter a bad time if the service was not as she thought it should be. That night they all ordered beef-burgers and french-fried potatoes.

With my friend wanting everything to be "just right," the french fries arrived *first*!

And they sat and sat and sat.

The people getting fidgety and the french fries getting cold and limp and tired, as is the way with french fries and people.

139

My friend began to look for the waitress. In her words . . . "I raised up in the booth and began to glare around the restaurant. After all, this was too much! My reflexes were all set to let her have it—in a nice refined way, of course. And then suddenly, I sank back down in my seat. Looking around the table at my guests, who had also been listening to you speak on Galatians 2:20, I fairly choked on my words, but I got it out: ' I can't let that waitress have it—I'm *dead!*' "

The good, easy laughter that is the Holy heritage of God's saints when they see suddenly what God is "up to," rippled around the auditorium where we met that morning with the crackle of a wood-fire and the roar of the Pacific somehow joining in.

From that woman's simple witness, twenty or thirty others who had not yet caught the truth of Galatians 2:20—began to laugh too. The relief *is* tremendous. *We can stop trying.*

We can even cease the struggle to cease struggling.

It has been done for us.

"We are crucified with Christ. . . ." "Knowing this, that our old man is crucified *with him.* . . ."

The part of that lady which could let fly at a waitress had been crucified with Christ. She had never before *dared* to take that fact by faith. And so it had not been hers. We only possess the gifts and promises of God as we take them for ourselves and dare to use them.

"Ye shall be my witnesses. . . ."

The "fried potatoes" witness was used of God to set others free that morning as the wood-fire crackled and the ocean kept on doing what it had been doing since the day He ". . . gave to the sea his decree . . ." and your witness can do the same. From now on.

You can quit longing for a victorious life and *have* it.

We have already been crucified with Christ. More than to "stop longing and die," we can stop longing and *know* that we are already *dead* to the down-pull of sin.

From the moment we *know* that because of what He did, we can stop longing and live!

17. STOP LONGING AND LIVE!

All life springs from death.

This is woven right into the fabric of the universe. We can't understand it. But we can recognize it all around us. We can see why Jesus said, ". . . Except a seed of corn fall into the ground and die, it abideth alone. . . ." We have all put seeds into the ground and have seen them appear again as living plants.

We have all seen seeds come from their little brown tombs.

This doesn't surprise anyone.

It follows the pattern we expect from nature as God made it. No one can explain the entrance of sin into the world. No one can fully explain why God permitted it to come. No one can fully understand how it is that by submitting Himself to death as Christ died on Calvary, God could so completely identify us with Himself that we too can know eternal life out of death.

We can't identify ourselves with God.

He must always make the first move toward us.

This is a great relief to me.

It is a still greater relief to know that He has already identified me with Himself both in death and in resurrection! The more I see my own helplessness and inadequacy the more relieved I am that this has already been done.

When Christ died, the uncontrollable part of me died too.

Seeing this is at the very base of freedom.

Power was let loose when Christ died. Dr. F. J. Huegel saw the connection between the graphic gospel account of Christ's death and sin in our lives. He describes the power let loose into the world from the place called Golgotha as a "kind of radium that kills" the tendency to sin in us! I too look in the gospel accounts and I find that when Jesus died, He cried in a *loud voice*, ". . . It is finished . . ."!

His life *built up* to death!

Other mere human lives dwindle toward death.

This power "to kill" is very real power. I find evidence of it wherever I need it and will take it. For a time after this aspect of the truth contained in Galatians 2:20 laid hold of me, I seemed to see reminders in the Bible of this power to kill and bring to life. Reminders in most unexpected places. God seemed almost to be shouting to me ". . . I know the thoughts that I think toward you . . . thoughts of peace, and not of evil, to give you an *expected* end."

He has every right to expect victory from us because He has already made it possible.

"See now that I, even I, am he, and there is no god with me: *I kill, and I make alive; I wound, and I heal. . . .*"

And again, *"The Lord killeth, and maketh alive*: he bringeth down to the grave, and bringeth up." ". . . he bringeth low, and lifteth up."

The way up is down.

Life springs from death.

A fact we are very, very slow to learn as Christians. A fact God will never tire of trying to show us. With all His heart I believe God *longs* for us to learn this elementary fact. Because He wants us to be truly free. Free of our grasping egos. And He knows that "dead men" require no attention!

He knows that dead women require no attention.

He knows we are free only when we are free of the bondage of self-protection and self-defense and self-pity and self-esteem. Only then can we really be trusted with life.

Only then would we know what to do with it.

But then we *can* know! Jesus Christ sets us free to live. Forever.

And well.

More about the art of living this new life in the next

chapter. But here, having accepted the fact that our troublesome nature or self, if you prefer, *has been* crucified with Christ, let's rejoice together for a few minutes that Paul inserted *this* thought *between* the two great facts in the first portion of this verse.

The first great fact is that we were crucified with Christ.

The second great fact is that Christ lives in us.

But, between these two is the glorious fact that *we are not extinguished*! We are *not* pushed into the dirt and forced to try to resemble worms when we were created in the image of God! I am forever convinced, that without Him I *can do nothing*. But I am also convinced that Jesus Christ didn't die in order to present the Father with redeemed worms or shattered vessels. He died to redeem men and women for God's use.

"I am crucified with Christ. . . ."

Yes.

And I rejoice in the fact that the old girl is dead!

But ". . . *nevertheless, I live* . . ."!

An "I" made whole and clean and acceptable to God *because* of what Jesus Christ did that day when the veil was torn from top to bottom. An "I" whose scars have been made radiant and whose useless years have been restored. Whose "old wastes" have been built.

Whose "former desolations" have been raised.

An "I" which has been given beauty for its own dry ashes. Oil for its abject mourning. A beautiful garment of praise for its death-bound spirit of heaviness. A *re-deemed* self *lifted* from the mire of self-destruction, and planted by the Lord Himself in the rich earth at the foot of His Own cross.

A self whose roots were washed by His blood.

Watered by His tears.

Redeemed . . . that I, *even I*, "might be called a tree of righteousness, the planting of the Lord, that *he* might be glorified."

That He might be glorified.

According to *His* purpose, you and I live that *He* might be glorified.

Is that according to our purpose too?

God does not intend to smash us into the ground and exalt Himself by beating us down. This is the very opposite of the good news Jesus came to announce!

God's intentions toward us are that we should have ". . . life and . . . have it more abundantly"! He took us to the cross with Him so He could plant us in the fertile soil of His Own life, spilled out on Calvary. His intentions are to tend us and water us and be our very growth!

"I am crucified with Christ . . ." (so that) I can live!

". . . nevertheless *I live.* . . ."

Christ died so that *you* might live!

In my cabin at a summer conference a shy, introverted little lady in her fifties sat telling me the tragic story of

146

her life. She was the colorless and unnoticed member of a rather brilliant and talented family. For years she carried her pain of feeling unwanted and it twisted her personality out of any resemblance to the one God intended her to have in the first place. Her very pain at being ignored made her more of a burden to her uncaring family. And so her heartache grew.

And when it had reached the breaking point at the tragic circumstances surrounding her father's death, she let it break at the foot of the cross of Jesus Christ. Being Jesus Christ, of course, He healed her heart. And I shall never forget the look on her plain, but radiant face as she said shyly, but with great certainty, "If no one else in all the world had needed a Saviour but me, Jesus would have died—just for me."

She was *experiencing* the wonder of the love of God. *For each one of us.*

She had discovered the secret at the heart of the gospel.

". . . Christ Jesus came into the world to *save* sinners. . . ."

If you are saved from something, you are *rescued.* Would He try to smash you into a nobody after what He did to rescue you? God is not quixotic. He is consistent.

He redeemed us to *use* us. Not to extinguish us.

Please do not misunderstand me. I do not mean to imply for one brief instant that God is to be thought of

147

as a Cosmic Servant to our special personality quirks! He is not "the first and the last" in order to guarantee me success in my new job.

He did not lay down His life that I might live in luxury.

But He has done something better.

He took my sinful self to the cross with Him so that I might live . . . but *not* as the old I. The Berkeley Version of the New Testament reads: "I am crucified jointly with Christ; I no longer live as I, but Christ lives within me."

". . . I no longer live *as I*. . . ."

". . . old things are passed away; behold, all things are become new."

". . . nevertheless I live. . . ." And I am learning more clearly everyday *how* to live. Why?

Because "Christ lives in me."

The One who created me in the beginning has made a way to come and live right *in me*! The One who knows *why* His very presence brings me unspeakable joy. He should know. He created me. The One who knows what my *true self* longs for, *has come in.*

The One who can fulfill every longing of my true self is here.

The One who can fulfill every longing of your true self is there living *in* you.

Not to squelch you. To *fulfill* you!

If you will relax in His presence, He will begin to give

you your heart's desire. Because only He knows what it is!

"I am he that liveth, and was dead; and, behold, I am alive for evermore . . ."!

And He is in you, if you have received Him.

You can . . . you *can* stop longing and live!

18. STOP LONGING AND LET LOVE LIVE!

The best definition of love I know is contained in the mighty three-word sentence John wrote in his first letter:

". . . God is love."

God, in the Person of Jesus Christ, is all we can know of love. It is all we need to know.

Love is the most attractive force in all the world. It is the most sought-after possession in all the world. Men may spend their lives seeking riches and fame, but when it comes time to die, they long for love, with a longing that even death cannot diminish!

We all long for it.

We were created that way.

Then, does that mean we all long for God?

If ". . . God *is* love." Yes.

And if the Bible is right and if my own experience of the love of God in Jesus Christ is valid, God *is* love. And I long for Him. So do you. You may not know it. I didn't for many, many years. But I now know that whether we recognize it or not, we all long for the love of God with a longing that cannot be measured or weighed. Except perhaps to measure it inversely by the size of the shrunken heart that beats without love and to weigh it against the paradox of the heavy heart where no love is.

As I understand it, the gospel of Jesus Christ tells us of the possibility of the miracle of the life of God *in us*!

By my reasoning, if God is love, and if He actually comes to be in us when we receive Him, then we can love according to the extent of His occupancy in our lives.

Is this reasonable?

If it is unreasonable and impossible, then why did Jesus say we were to love our neighbors as we love ourselves? He recognized our "selves" in this great commandment. Christ Himself tells me He does not intend to extinguish me. He wants to fill me with His very life and thereby change my self so that it begins to resemble His lovely self.

He will be my very capacity and ability and power to love.

Without Him living His Own life in me, there are some people I simply could *never* love! I tried for years with two or three of them and the relief was great when I found it was just impossible for *me*. But it is not impossible for Him. His very nature is love.

Mine isn't.

But His is.

Is it natural for me to love everyone?

No.

Is it natural for me to love everyone as much as I love myself?

No.

But the One whom I seek to follow tells me that I *must* love my neighbor as much as I love myself.

This is not natural at all.

But it is *super*natural, and possible because He will come and live His Own lovely life right in me.

"I am crucified with Christ: nevertheless I live; yet not I, but *Christ liveth in me. . . .*"

I am still living. I am still to be reckoned with, both by my friends and by God. I still have a self. The part of that self which *prefers* to defy God was crucified. The false, selfish "I" was killed on the cross. When I lay hold of this fact by faith, it becomes mine. I find that the next time I want to assert myself because that old groove is still worn in my brain from such long usage, I don't *have* to do to do it any more!

Dead people require no attention.

They don't need to have the center of the floor.

They don't need to defend themselves.

But, I rejoice to know God has not snuffed me out.

". . . nevertheless I live. . . ."

". . . yet not I (as the old I), but *Christ liveth in me*. . . ."

There is Someone else living here now too!

We are together in a tender, closeness that is One.

We love each other.

I am His and He is mine.

But more than that we live as One.

Which means we can also *love* as One.

This is not true in its most complete sense with us all. Some of us have only partial union with Christ. This is not His idea. It is ours. He wants to be entirely One with us as He and the Father are One. But some of us have not placed our selves under His complete mastery. And, when we have not, there is no reason to expect that we will behave or think or react as though we have! No reason to expect that we will love everyone. We still have the right *not* to love those who do not appeal to us if we are still partially in command of our selves. Even of our redeemed selves.

Galatians 2:20 is the most perfect definition of the Christian life. It is not a goal to be reached. It is a witness to make because of what He has worked out for us.

Paul is simply saying that Christ took Saul to the cross and set Paul free to live. He is simply declaring that he, Paul, has learned the art of real living *because* he has surrendered his entire self to Christ's occupancy and therefore he is living fully because Christ *in* Paul knows *how* to live!

Who else would know as Christ would know?

"In him *is* life. . . ."

"I am the . . . life. . . ."

The Creator of life and life itself.

When He comes in, life comes in and we come under the influence and the control of the One who thought it all up in the beginning!

". . . without him was not any thing made that was made."

He Himself is my very life.

He Himself is your very life.

If He is not, He wants to be.

The world says, "Realize *yourself.*" The modern cults of self-development say, "Realize the good in yourself."

Jesus Christ says: ". . . whosoever will *lose* his life for *my* sake, the same shall save it."

The cults say in accord with the voice of the world: "Realize your God-life already present in you."

Jesus says: "Lose your sinful life for my sake."

"I will *then* come and live My Own life right in you."

". . . as many as *received* him, to them gave he power to become the sons of God. . . ."

When we receive Him, He comes in.

Bringing His power, His faith, His abiding, His peace, His very life.

Bringing Himself.

And ". . . it pleased the Father that *in him* should all fulness dwell."

If you have been trying to declare the "Christ in you" and have never received Him, you are trying to beat down the door of heaven with your poor fists!

Receive Him as best you know how right now and He will come in. The capacity for Him is there. The longing is there. The emptiness is there. The big empty space created to fit *only* the Person of the Lord Jesus Christ was created right in you when you were created. But even if you are also sincerely trying to "declare sin away," it remains and keeps His life *out*, until He Himself has forgiven it. Denying does not get rid of sin. That is done only by the blood of Jesus Christ. The cross is not a symbol of our need to do the best we can to live a sacrificial life, thinking of others and doing good deeds. The cross is not a symbol. The cross was very *real*. The blood He shed there was very *real*.

And it is the only *real* way to be rid of the sinful self in us all which keeps His life out because He is a Holy God. Receive Him as your Saviour from sin and He will forgive your sin and come in.

155

Whether you believe it or not, ". . . all have sinned. . . ."

That isn't my idea. It is God's.

If this is the very first Christian book you have ever read, you can still turn right now and receive His life into yours, when you confess your need of a Saviour.

Very few seem to know this.

Very few seem to know that the Christian life is not merely a way to be good, or to find fellowship with other human beings whose hearts also long. Very few seem to realize that a Christian is not one who can snap his prayer-fingers and God will obey. Few seem to realize that being a Christian is not simply being sure you are going to whatever you conceive as heaven.

Or not going to whatever you conceive as hell.

Very few seem to know that being a Christian is Christ living in us right now!

A Christian is one in whom Jesus Christ lives *now*.

". . . the life which I now live in the flesh I live by the faith of the Son of God, who loved me, and gave himself for me." Our Galatians 2:20 has a mighty ending!

"I am crucified with Christ: nevertheless I live; yet not I, but Christ liveth in me: *and the life which I now live in the flesh* I live by the faith of the Son of God, who loved me, and gave himself for me."

A Christian is one in whom Christ lives *now*.

Think who He is!

Shouldn't we be wonderful people?

Look who lives in us.

". . . without him was not any thing made that was made." The One who lives in us is the One before whom one day ". . . every knee shall bow. . . ."

He is the first and the last.

". . . the name which is above every name. . . ."

". . . Wonderful, Counsellor, The mighty God, The everlasting Father, The Prince of Peace!"

The Lord, Jesus Christ!

In me?

In you?

Yes.

Then why are we as we are? Why are we such poor examples of what a Christian can be? Why do the pagans down the block have every right to laugh at our Christianity?

Why are we so often unlike the One who is living His very life *in us*?

Just as we have never laid hold of the fact that we were already crucified with Him, so we have never let it break all the way into our consciousness that *He does live in us*!

We operate from another point altogether.

We operate from the point of one, "trying-to-be-humble" earth-bound creature looking longingly to a far-away, benevolent, but distant God.

We are here and He is there.

It is true that Jesus Christ in His glorified body does sit at the right hand of the Father, "ever living to make intercession for us." But by a mystery which we don't even need to try to understand, this same Christ also comes to live His life again *in us*.

God incarnate again, walking the face of this old earth in us!

Incredible?

Yes. But true. And possible.

And it will show too, *when* we have taken this fact and made it ours. When we have begun to *let* Him not only do the acting but the *reacting* for us!

If you've received Him, He's there in you. He wants to bring you into such an indescribably close union with Himself that your very reactions will become His. His will become yours.

Do I understand this?

No.

But I have experienced it. And during the time I experience it, during the time I lose myself in Him willingly, I know I am not only learning the art of true living, I know I am being lived through by the One who created life.

By the One who is life.

Do I experience this consistently?

I experience this victorious life consistently *according to how much I depend upon His never failing me!*

". . . I will never leave thee, nor forsake thee."

I have His Word for that.

". . . lo, I am with you alway. . . ."

That is the last thing He said before He ascended bodily to sit at the right hand of the Father until all things will be put under His feet. It is as though, if we forget everything else, He longed to have us remember that He would never leave us.

"I will always be right there with you. In you."

". . . if any man . . . open the door . . . I will come in. . . ."

But, you ask, "How does this work out in my daily life? *How* do I begin to live this victorious life? *How* do I begin to give Christ freedom to live in me?"

Examples from real life are always best.

My friend, Ellen, does our grocery shopping. Our meat is always excellent, and so I asked her if she held a special charm over the boys at the butcher counter.

"No," she replied. "I've just heard the other women fly at the poor butchers day in and day out and I simply take Galatians 2:20 very literally every time I walk in the store. I let Christ talk to the boys behind the counter *for me!*"

159

The glory here is that, even if the meat should be tough and too fat, *He* would never "fly at" the boys who sell it. Even if they weighed both thumbs with it, He would still be Himself.

Our meat is always good.

The real freedom comes, however, in no longer *needing* to feel "put upon" if it happens to be poor!

Nothing changes Jesus Christ and He will still be *in us.*

My very dear friend, Dr. Norman B. Harrison, whose writings and life have done so much to assure me that I am being shown the *true* light in Galatians 2:20, quite unknowingly gave me another magnificent demonstration of Christ in us when I first came to know him in the summer of 1955. Of course, I had heard of Dr. Harrison, and had met him once briefly. But at the Mound Keswick Conference that summer we were both speakers.

Before I had read a word he had written, before I had heard even one of his power-filled messages, he came up to me, his face radiant beneath his wavy white hair and as he grasped both my hands, he said:

"Now, Genie, we're going to live love here this week, aren't we?"

Conference speakers often have interesting talks together at mealtime, and I had met some of God's great men and women here and there across the country. But this was different.

160

Christ Himself came up to me in Dr. Harrison and took both my hands and said: "Now, Genie, we're going to live love here this week, aren't we?"

He seemed to gather us all to take part in a new game of joy!

I could see his face, still handsome, shine with the very light of God as he sat that week patiently listening to me share what God had taught me firsthand from Galatians 2:20. He, a greatly venerated, highly educated Bible expositor . . . I, merely a witness. But it was as though God and Brother Norman sat there listening together sharing a big, shining secret!

God was *in* that dear old man.

And the more I saw of him during that week the more I was convinced that the great discovery of my life had been made! It *was* possible, just as it had come to me from that verse, to live an ordinary life right here on this earth, in *complete union* with and under the *complete control* of Christ! Dr. Harrison's messages thrilled me. Our brief conversations here and there on the grounds were charged with eternity. Each day as I spoke I became more and more convinced. Dr. Harrison seemed to be a man filled with the *delights* and the energy of God. At eighty he was sure and joyful and his face shone. It was as though he had just then discovered God himself!

From the pulpit and at dinner and on the grounds he fairly radiated joy. I wondered about his family. His daughter, Marjorie, was with him and I couldn't help thinking what real fun they must have together! How happy their home life must be.

I wondered if Dr. Harrison had ever known deep sorrow.

Almost everyone else knew already about his life. I, being such a new acquaintance, did not know. I was just taken up with the fact that *in him*, God was showing me the joy of heaven itself.

And then, on the last day I learned, quite by accident, that the dear old fellow was there proclaiming the good news and *living* it before us only a *few weeks* after the tragic death of his beloved daughter, Frances, with whom he had worked for twenty years . . . *and* only a *few days* after the death of his wife!

I was jolted and the jolt sent me still deeper into the truth of Galatians 2:20.

I *knew* Christ lived in Dr. Harrison.

His books and his preaching were filled with the authority of God Himself, but Brother Norman's *life* showed me what I needed to see.

I *saw* Christ controlling his entire being and showing forth His joy which sorrow cannot dim. Even this old man's grieving heart was lit with the joy of heaven.

A few months later in Chicago I watched the same Christ take over in Brother Norman's *reactions* when a friend of mine inadvertently picked up the wrong brief case as he took Dr. Harrison to a train. I knew that brief case was the most important piece of luggage he had. The time element made it impossible for him to receive it for at least three days. The same Christ was still living in him and my friend, a comparatively new Christian, was neither hurt nor made to feel humiliated at his careless mistake.

Jesus Christ never hurts anyone.

He goes along right *in us* to the grocery store, to the conference ground, through sorrow, through the minor annoyances, and He will also love that person whom you simply cannot love!

A sincere Christian woman found she had never really let Him *love* through her until her mother-in-law came to live with her. The mother-in-law could easily have been the model for all cartoons and the evil inspiration for all stories about mothers-in-law. We looked at Galatians 2:20 together as we walked across a college campus one day. She *saw it* and this is what she said:

"Well, it's a relief to know I can't love her! To know I don't have to. That He will love her through me."

We just walked along for a moment and then she said, in a voice that was almost childlike in its discovery, "My mother-in-law is very old. She'll be bed-fast one of these days and then I can really let Him take care of her through me!"

When we first began to walk, she wanted me to com-

163

miserate with her. The instant she began to *accept* her wretched situation and to dare to think He would do the loving through her, His very presence within her began to influence her entire outlook! He was there all the time. Before she talked to me. Apparently she had forgotten it. Or hadn't known that she could depend upon Him entirely!

Love was living right in her!

Waiting to love even her mother-in-law *through* her.

Another woman, a dear friend, struggling painfully through the heavy humiliation of having her husband divorce her after thirty years of married life, allowed this great truth of His indwelling presence to take hold of *her,* and even though the husband went through with the divorce, even though everyone in the town knew it, even though they also knew about the other woman, my friend won two of her four embittered daughters to Christ by letting them see Christ *hold her* and *react for her* and *love through her* as they went through this ghastly ordeal together.

This woman is alone now. Her big, lovely home is very empty at times. But *she* is not empty. Her humor is strong, she can laugh at herself, she gives of herself and lives a full and creative life.

Her circumstances did not change.

But Christ living in her, changed *her.*

She fell completely under His influence! And they became One forever.

164

"I am crucified with Christ. . . ."

". . . nevertheless I live. . . ."

". . . Yet not I, but Christ liveth in me . . ."!

Don't be afraid to make it yours. We can, oh, we can stop longing for love, stop longing to be able to love the unlovely. We *can* stop longing and let love Himself live *in us*!

19. DAVID LONGED

"David longed. . . ."

David, who had all his life been handsome and courageous and daring in battle and in thought . . .

David, whose talent upon the harp rivaled his talent to create poems of praise to enlarge his melodies . . .

David, praised and adored by the women who ". . . came out of all cities of Israel, singing and dancing . . ." to the lilt and laud of their adulation of David, who had ". . . slain . . . his ten thousands."

David, popular enough to stir the jealousy of a king . . . beloved by one whose human love bore a shadow of the great heart that broke on Calvary. ". . . the soul of Jonathan was knit with the soul of David, and Jonathan *loved him as his own* soul." David, sharing the very soul of a man who had every reason to hate him, but who instead ". . . stripped himself of the robe that was upon him, and gave it to David, and his garments, even to his sword, and to his bow and to his girdle."

David, the skillful shepherd boy who slew a giant, became a prince's friend and then himself king, anointed of God, mighty in battle and gentle in spirit, leader of "mighty men," called by God Himself "a man after God's Own heart" . . . this David, of the house of Jesse, from whose line was to come Christ Himself.

This David—*longed.*

Surrounded by his "mighty men," headquartered in the cave of Adullam, King David *longed.*

The Philistines "pitched in the valley" between, held his beloved native city of Bethlehem. King David and his "mighty men" were cut off and waiting in their cave for a chance to attack and regain the city beloved to David.

But David did not speak of his longing for Bethlehem itself.

He did something any one of us might have done.

Sitting there, as he was, surrounded by his strong followers, instead of speaking in mighty phrases of mighty military plans to be carried out by "mighty men," David did what we might have done.

David longed for a drink of water from an old well he loved.

". . . David longed, and said, Oh that one would

167

give me drink of the water of the well of Bethlehem, which is by the gate"!

How many times have you, if you have ever drunk water from a well near a place you loved, longed for one drink of that particular well-water? Perhaps you "taste" it from a gourd, as I remember water from the well on my Uncle Steve's farm. Perhaps you "taste" it from a tin cup. But when you long for that water, is it really the water for which you long?

Is it really the *water* for which you long?

Isn't it rather a longing to recapture something you have lost? Isn't it rather a longing to hold again, or perhaps to capture for the first time something you meant to grasp and never let go when you stood by that old well all those long years ago?

Is it really the water you want?

Or is it that "feeling" you had as you drank the water?

Could it be that your heart longs to "go back" and look more closely along the road of the years that lead from that well to now?

Did you lose something along the way?

Would you like to go back and look for it?

Or did you step on a clump of violets as you walked indifferently away from the well the last time? And would you like to go back and straighten them up again and loosen the black earth around their roots and give them a chance to begin to grow once more?

168

Is it the *water* for which you long?

Or is it the peace you knew back in that uncomplicated time when you stood there drinking and thinking about nothing at all?

Is it the *water* you want, or the chance to "make up" for something you crushed?

Is it the water you want, or the peace you knew as you drank it?

Is it childhood?

Is it your parents you long for?

Is it rest? Art thou "wearied in the greatness of thy way"?

In the length of the journey?

Or is your life going by so fast your heart cries out for time to taste it as you used to taste that clean, cold water at the well?

Are you anxious and frightened by the flying-by of all the things you hold dear? Would you like to hold them all for just a clear, peace-washed moment as you held that water in that green- and yellow-striped gourd by that old well where once you drank?

Are you longing for a higher place, above the dirt and smoke of your own failures and defeats? Or above the dirt and smoke of too much success?

Do you perhaps long for your heart to be mended?

Or for a return to the simplicity of a humble heart?

Is it really the *water* you want?

Or do you long to be free again? As free as you were the days you drank at that well?

Do you long to be wanted once more as you knew you were wanted when you drank the clean, clear water from the well which belonged to someone who belonged to you too? To whom you belonged?

Is there a battle up ahead from where you wait now? And are you sitting there in the temporary protection of your "cave of Adullam" trying to escape what's up ahead by longing for what was so precious to you once?

Is there a parting up ahead?

An ending of all you hold dear?

Are you putting off the future by "putting on" the past?

Even for a moment?

The moment you'd need to drink just one tin cup of water from an old well?

Is it really the water for which you longed?

Was it really the water for which David longed?

Perhaps the answer lies in the finish of that little story about David and his "mighty men" as they waited there in the interim cave of Adullam.

"And David longed, and said, Oh that one would give me drink of the water of the well of Bethlehem, which is by the gate! And the three mighty men brake through the host of the Philistines, and drew water out of the well of Bethlehem, that was by the gate, and took it, and brought it to David: *nevertheless he would not drink thereof, but poured it out unto the Lord.*"

David would not drink the precious water, after his faithful men had risked their lives to bring it to him.

". . . David longed . . . (and then) poured it out unto the Lord"!

Why did David do this?

Was the water *too precious* because it had come to him at the risk of the very lives of the men who loved him and whom he loved?

Yes. Certainly this was one reason.

I know this was one reason because this little story of David and his pitcher of water from the well at Bethlehem has been one of the main melody lines of my entire Christian life!

And for three or four years of that life, it caused me to learn the higher way of giving back to the Lord as a love-offering, memories of my old life which were still precious to me—but less than God's best. I "poured out" my work over and over again. My desire to play god in my own life. Intellectual concepts which had found such wide welcome in my mind through the years in which I *did* "play god" in my own life. I "poured out" certain music which caused me to reach for the tattered graveclothes I still trailed. Music that made me want to

171

pull those graveclothes close around me again and hide in their dark, still familiar folds. Still familiar and dear because I had hidden there so long before He rolled the stone away and called me to come out and live!

For these dark hiding places I sometimes longed.

They were familiar and I had lived in them a long time.

But I knew the stone was rolled away. He *had* come in. And more often I found gladness in "pouring out" to Him even the memories of things I once held dear before morning came. More often I found gladness and always I found release.

And more Oneness with Him.

If you have been a Christian since you were very young, you may not understand clinging to old things. But here and there in the world are others who like myself, experienced the new birth as adults, and who have been enabled at crisis times to take God's power to resist temptation because they knew David's "water story" had worked for me.

Thoughts can be "poured out."

Habits can be "poured out."

Longings can be "poured out."

A young man now in the service of His Lord confided that although his mind and heart were forever turned toward Christ, he still suffered agonies of longing for alcohol. I reminded him of David and his precious water. When the boy wants a drink now, he "pours out his longing unto the Lord."

And the Lord sets him free of it.

Perhaps you are asking: "Is alcohol precious?"

Yes. It is the most precious thing in the world to the alcoholic! And if God took our sin, surely He will take the outward manifestation of it which has become precious to a man whose values and concepts were twisted by the very sin God died to cleanse away.

This "pouring out unto the Lord" has helped narcotic addicts who have turned to Christ. It has helped those who have been forced to give up work they loved because the work somehow was against God.

The time comes, in most instances, when the freedom is constant.

Only now and then do I have to "pour out unto the Lord" something still dear to me from my old life. The new grooves are formed in our brains. "Old things"— and that means old grooves in our brains too—"are passed away."

Memories remain, however, and memories can make us long.

We need not fear them.

We need not be ashamed or let Satan's super-weapon of discouragement defeat us because our desires are not as "spiritual" as we think they should be! I almost "went under" on that one once. Until a saint named Anna Mow said: "So what if you're the one who wrote *Discoveries* and *The Burden Is Light*? You weren't witnessing to yourself, were you? You were witnessing to Jesus Christ!"

I saw her point and Holy laughter came back.

Directed toward *me*.

I had expected too much of my "spiritual self"!

Expect *everything* of Christ *in you*.

But *nothing* of yourself.

And don't fret if you have to continue "pouring out unto the Lord" that one thing which trips you on your way. Or those several things.

Just be glad there is that way to do it!

If you are trying to quit drinking, and you have *already* received Jesus Christ as your Saviour, the next time you think you're going to die if you don't have a drink—the next time you even think of a drink—"pour the longing out unto the Lord!"

This method has worked wonders for me with food too.

And with as many others as are willing to try it!

Not only am I losing the last several pounds which keep me from being a "fit temple" for the Holy Spirit, I am finding still another way of communion with the One I love.

The next time a forbidden dish is passed your way, give it to the Lord as a love-offering! Your craving for chocolate pie or black-eyed peas may not cause as much social disturbance or cost quite as much money as the

174

alcoholic's craving for liquor, but it springs from the same twisted source. You're "taking out" an emotional lack in your life—trying to satisfy a *longing* with pie!

The alcoholic is trying to satisfy an emotional longing with whiskey.

Both escape into the temporary oblivion of self-satisfaction as the liquor and the pie go down!

Perhaps you say you have a sweet tooth and you can't help it.

The alcoholic has a physical as well as emotional longing for liquor too. Of himself he can't help it either.

None of this is the point. *God can help in both cases.*

God can give you complete victory from chocolate pie and bourbon! I have seen the same glint of defiance in the eyes of an overweight housewife *and* a chronic alcoholic when it is mentioned that God can change them *both* so much they will no longer *need* to eat that extra "snack" of solid calories of an afternoon or take even one more drink throughout all eternity!

The glint comes when neither one wants *total* freedom.

But when we do want it—from anything, we can have it by pouring out unto the Lord, the specific thing or relationship or circumstance to which we cling in our frantic efforts to assuage our longings.

If you feel forsaken, unwanted, "pour it out unto the Lord." *Be willing* to thank Him for your very feeling of loneliness because each time you "pour it out" before

Him, you experience His love in a deeper way. You belong to each other more completely than you did the moment before. You may not feel this each time. But it will be true. I cannot explain it, but there is a law involved here.

And it always works.

If you are lonely, remember "God setteth the solitary in families . . . but the rebellious dwell in a dry land." Alone. If we rebel at our lot, we dwell alone. If we make a love-offering of our heartache to God, ". . . the Lord will take (us) up." Unto Himself.

Our personality twists will disappear as we praise Him and build our tottering altars before Him, and soon our loneliness will be gone because when He is living fully within us, we *attract* other people. "Christ in me" . . . my only hope of companionship. He draws. He will draw to me, *when* I have cheerfully laid down my loneliness and heartache as a love-offering at His dear feet.

". . . I, if I be lifted up . . . will draw. . . ."

We are beginning to move into a new and deeper meaning of this story of David's water "poured out unto the Lord."

We all long.

David longed.

Only the neurotic or the self-righteous deny it.

We twist our longings until the things for which we long are not what God would choose. But the longing itself is from God. He gives the ability to long. And when we long for something precious to *us*, even if it is sinful in God's sight, He will *take* that thing as a love-offering *from* us, *if* we will "pour it out unto Him."

He will take it and redeem it and give it back *changed* into what He alone knows will satisfy the true longing in us. The longing which always comes from Him.

From His heart to our hearts.

He will always take the "precious thing" we offer, even if it is sinful, because *we* are precious to Him!

Calvary is here.

Here the cross is raised in your particular circumstance.

There He *took* the thing so "precious" to man—self-rule!

Bondage to self.

Sin.

And set man free.

So, He will take *whatever* you are willing to "pour out" unto Him.

But there is more here for us.

If the lonely person pours out his loneliness *with thanksgiving* for the loneliness itself, God not only receives the offering, He gloriously *transforms* the one who has "poured it out," however tremblingly. He *transforms* the one who gave thanks, however feebly.

I am just learning this.

My dear friend, Ethel Wilcox, helped me see it first.

Her only son, whom she loved so deeply, was killed in the Second World War. Walking together back to our rooms, across the grounds at the Mound Keswick Conference, where we were both speaking, I said: "You've really had a chance to try Him, haven't you?"

Her smile was radiant, and her voice was quiet with the deep things of God, as she replied: "Yes, I've had so much in which to *give thanks!*"

"Giving thanks always for *all things.* . . ."

This too is a law woven right into the fabric of the spiritual life.

Her victorious life proves it.

So can yours if you are willing not only to "pour out unto the Lord" that thing which causes your longing, but to give thanks for the *need* to come to Him in such a deep way.

If your heart is broken, lay it at His feet and give thanks for the broken heart. He will heal it and He will show you how blessed you are above those who live as dully as though they have no hearts!

If you are in confusion, "pour it out unto the Lord" and thank Him for that particular confusion, because if it had not come to you, you would not be seeking Him as you seek Him now!

If you are defeated, make a love-offering of your defeat to the Lord. And give thanks that you failed. Because if you had not failed you may never have discovered the life-changing truth that without Him you can do nothing!

Give thanks for your *need,* as you "pour it out unto the Lord."

Without it, you may never have sought Him as you seek Him now.

20. EARLY WILL I SEEK THEE!

David longed.

David, a man after God's own heart, longed with a longing that sprang from the very heart of the God who chose him.

"Ye have not chosen me, but I have chosen you. . . ."

David longed as we long.

God has also chosen us. All of us.

And His great heart longs to have us for His Own. This is also too high for me. I cannot attain to it. But I know that it is true.

David longed for water from the well at Bethlehem. But when he got it, he "poured it out unto the Lord."

Because it was precious to David.

And also because, as with you as you long for a drink from another old well, he did not really want the *water* itself. He wanted what the water meant to him.

He wanted what he had missed being away from where the water was.

He longed for what still lived in his heart concerning that water.

He longed for the *source* of the water.

"O God, thou art my God; early will I seek thee: my soul thirsteth for thee, my flesh longeth for thee in a dry and thirsty land, where no water is."

This same David, earlier in his life, hiding under the wilderness night-sky from his enemy, Saul, called from the depths of his already thirsty soul for the source of the water he needed so much in that "dry and thirsty land where no water was!"

"O God, thou art my God. . . ."

"My soul thirsteth for *thee*. . . ."!

And God called back as He calls now . . . "Ho, everyone that thirsteth, come ye to the waters. . . ."

". . . If *any* man thirst, let him come unto *me* and drink . . . whosoever drinketh of the water that I shall give him shall never thirst; but the water that I shall give him shall be in him a well of water springing up into everlasting life."

David longed. And his longing came from God and was for God Himself.

"O God, thou art my God; early will I seek thee: my soul thirsteth for thee, my flesh longeth for thee in a dry and thirsty land, where no water is; To see thy power and thy glory, so as I have seen thee in the sanctuary. Because thy lovingkindness is better than life, my lips shall praise thee."

David longed for God Himself.

He knew God.

~~And almost the instant he cried out~~ for more of the ~~Lord, Himself, this same Lord flooded David's heart with the secret of the "~~. . . ~~well of water~~ springing up into ~~everlasting life."~~ When David began to cry out for more of *God*, almost immediately he was caused to remember God's lovingkindness and that it ". . . is better than life."

God showed David alone out there in the wilderness what the inside of His heart was like. And at once, David began to praise Him!

"Because thy lovingkindness is better than life, my lips shall praise thee. Thus will I bless thee while I live: I will lift up my hands in thy name."

David's longing came from God.

David's longing was for God Himself.

And that longing was satisfied the instant David began to *praise* God and to *bless* Him.

"My soul shall be satisfied as with marrow and fatness; and my mouth shall praise thee with joyful lips; When I remember thee upon my bed, and meditate on thee in the night watches."

David praised Him out there alone in the wilderness in extreme danger at the hands of his enemy. And instinctively he knew he would be praising Him when once more he lay upon his bed at night in safety.

But what of the "night watches" during which we lie

182

upon our beds in physical safety but in mental anguish? A woman whose husband had just died told me her most agonizing times were alone at night in the dark . . . in the empty house . . . empty of her loved one . . . empty of sleep for her. Alone. Then one night she began to praise Him and to read aloud David's heart-cry . . .

"O God, thou art my God . . . my soul thirsteth for thee . . . because thy lovingkindness is better than life, my lips shall praise thee."

When at last her heart was turned to Him in gratitude for Himself, her burning grief began to subside. And although her nights remained sleepless for some time, soon she was able to "meditate on Him in the night watches." Peacefully and quietly, without rebellion or fear at being left alone.

She was not alone.

She was *enabled* to cry "O God, thou art my God; early will I seek *thee* . . ." because He was there seeking more of her.

As He is there, seeking more of you.

As He is here, seeking more of me.

And He will never stop seeking. His is the shepherd nature. He longs for all His sheep to be safe at home.

~~David longed. But he also sang . . . "The Lord is my shepherd; I shall not want" for anything which He Himself cannot supply.~~

~~David longed.~~

~~I long.~~

You are longing and God is longing to give you Himself in the Person of the indwelling Christ. When He comes in, ~~and as you receive Him by faith,~~ your every longing ~~will~~ *can* be met. Because ". . . it pleased the Father that in him should all fulness dwell."

He Himself will be your salvation.

He Himself will be your growth.

He Himself will be your faith.

He Himself will be your constancy.

Your peace.

Your sensitivity, your objectivity, your simplicity, your originality.

Jesus Christ, Himself, will show you what God is really like.

Will give you a look at the very face of God Himself!

He will make you new. He will teach you how to meet suffering and failure. He will teach you that He has already taken your uncontrollable self to the cross when He went to the cross. As He is teaching me.

Jesus Christ, living in you, will not only teach you how to live fully, He will live His life *through* you. He will love you and He will love *for* you.

He will fill your every longing. As He is filling mine. *But*, there is more.

He *will* satisfy your every true longing with Himself, but He will also, when the time is right for *you,* create in you a still deeper longing beside which all others pale.

184

If you do not see this yet, wait upon Him to show you when it is time.

You may find no words to express it, other than the words David found. But the longing will be new and it will flame white-hot in your heart until you cry, as I cry, once more and still once more . . . and yet once more . . .

"O God, thou art my God; early will I seek thee. . . ."

And when it "comes to pass about the spring of the day" that you are yet seeking Him in still dryer land, "lift up your hands in His name" And give thanks, because the One who created your *new longing,* has done it because He longs for more of *you.*

As He longs to give you more of Himself.

And more. And still more.

"O God, thou art my God; early will I seek thee: my soul thirsteth for thee, my flesh longeth for thee in a dry and thirsty land where no water is."

"O God, thou art my God . . . early will I seek— *thee. . . .*"

CPSIA information can be obtained
at www.ICGtesting.com
Printed in the USA
JSHW030513250221
12032JS00001BA/37